P9-EDM-963

WITHDRAWN
UTSA Libraries

# The Big Question

# POETS ON POETRY · Donald Hall, General Editor

*David Lehman*

# The Big Question

Ann Arbor

THE UNIVERSITY OF MICHIGAN PRESS

Copyright ©1995 by David Lehman
All rights reserved
Published in the United States of America by
The University of Michigan Press
Manufactured in the United States of America
⊗Printed on acid-free paper
1998   1997   1996   1995   4   3   2   1

*A CIP catalogue record for this book is available from the British Library.*

Library of Congress Cataloging-in-Publication Data

Lehman, David, 1948–
  The big question / David Lehman.
    p.   cm. — (Poets on poetry)
    ISBN 0-472-09583-8 (hardcover : alk. paper). — ISBN
0-472-06583-1 (paper : alk. paper)
    1. Lehman, David, 1948—Aesthetics.  2. American literature—
20th century—History and criticism—Theory, etc.  3. Literature,
Modern—History and criticism—Theory, etc.  4. Postmodernism
(Literature) 5. Books—Reviews. 6. Poetry.  I. Title.  II. Series.
PS3562.E428B54   1995
814'.54—dc20                                              95-5493
                                                              CIP

Library
University of Texas
at San Antonio

*Oh, do not ask, "What is it?"*
*Let us go and make our visit.*

—T. S. Eliot, "The Love Song of J. Alfred Prufrock"

*for Donald Hall*

# Contents

## Part 4 Criticism and Controversy

# Preface

Most of the essays and articles in this book were written in the last three years. I wrote them not with a book in mind but in response to an editor's call, an invitation to give a lecture, or a request for an essay. There are pieces here on Philip Larkin and on Philip Roth, on a great Australian poetry hoax, and on Charles Dickens's mysteriously unfinished last novel. Recurrent themes include the scandalous behavior of European philosophers, the predicaments of biographers, and the phenomenon of poetry "slams" and the whole "spoken word" scene in downtown bars. The essays that raise big questions—postmodernism, deconstruction, political correctness—help organize the articles around them by setting out some principal terms of discussion. There are also a couple of satirical poems, an op-ed column, and a bunch of book reviews. A few are ardent. People cite Randall Jarrell for his devastating putdowns and no-punches-pulled reviews, but it should be remembered, too, that he wrote some gloriously enthusiastic appreciations. You read Jarrell on Whitman, and you want to rush out and read Whitman aloud from the rooftops.

It has seemed important to me, in the last few years, to distinguish postmodernism in art and culture from poststructuralism in academe. I have written critically and with polemic force against deconstruction. It is conceivable that deconstruction could be treated as a special instance of postmodernism, but this strikes me as a debater's trick. The continuities between John Ashbery's poetry and Jacques Derrida's "grammatology" are tenuous and impose no obligation: the reader is free to admire one and despise (or ignore) the other. I see no reason to pull down an edifice because a pillar offends my eyes. My attitude toward postmodernism is, as it is bound to be, complex and ambivalent. (Anything else would scarcely be appropriate to the spirit of postmodernism.) The term *postmodernism* itself is so mustily academic, I would avoid it if I could. Yet its value is undeniable for understanding many of the vital signs in our literary culture—including, for example, the novels of Philip Roth and Cynthia Ozick, not to mention the Australian poetry hoax and *The Mystery of Edwin Drood,* which are discussed in Part Two of this book.

Much of postmodernism can be understood as an anti-monumental monument to Janus, the two-faced god. I warm to the richness of irony in some postmodernist works. Irony acts as a restraint on passion that paradoxically sharpens and augments the passion. Being an ironist, I ought to point out that irony seems in some ways foreign to me, an Englishman's birthright not an American's. The English writer Alan Bennett has said about his national inheritance: "Irony is inescapable. We're conceived in irony. We float in it from the womb. It's the amniotic fluid. It's the silver sea. It's the waters at their priestlike task washing away guilt and purpose and responsibility. Joking but not joking. Caring but not caring. Serious but not serious." The American temperament is brash and earnest, not resigned. That temperamental difference is one reason why the ways and means of irony recommend themselves to an American writer. It is, at the least, a shrewd rhetorical move to write against the grain of your convictions or your passions. Irony is not whimsy. It is, on the contrary, a condition of high mental alertness, and it may be the most undervalued and misunderstood quality in contemporary poetry.

I want to thank the magazine editors who published these pieces and, in many cases, added value to them. These include Alida Becker, John Blades, Don Bruckner, Gail Caldwell, Michael Dirda, Dianne Donovan, David Fenza, Phillip Gourevich, John Homans, Richard Howard, Alan Jenkins, Larry Kart, Louise Kennedy, William Phillips, Alex Raksin, Rebecca Sinkler, Jeremy Treglown, and Jane Uscilka. "Deconstruction after the Fall" was presented at the Alabama Symposium on English and American Literature at the University of Alabama in October 1992. My thanks go to Dwight Eddins, who organized the event. "What Is It? The Question of Postmodernism" was delivered as a Taft Lecture at the University of Cincinnati in November 1994. I am grateful to Michael Atkinson, James Cummins, and Andrew Hudgins of the University of Cincinnati. In an earlier form the essay was presented at the inaugural session of the Bennington Writing Seminars in January 1994, and I want to thank Liam Rector, John Lane, and other Bennington friends for their help. Glen Hartley and Lynn Chu have, as always, advised me well. Monique Fowler's opinions were invaluable. Linda Howe copyedited with her usual deft touch. LeAnn Fields made everything go so smoothly. Without grants I received from the Lila Wallace-Reader's Digest Fund and from the Ingram Merrill Foundation, I could not have written this book. I would not have done so without the encouragement of Donald Hall.

*The Big Question* is dedicated to Don Hall for another reason. It was he who set up the series in which this book appears. Now forty-nine volumes strong, the Poets on Poetry series of the University of Michigan Press is a truly distinguished publishing venture, a record of the critical thinking of our leading poets. Don Hall has run the series with enthusiasm and generosity and discernment and care. He seems to be an expert at carving a tight book out of a shapeless manuscript. The remarkable thing is that he has done this work while doing so much else: poetry and essays and sports journalism, anthologies and textbooks, stories, biographies. Don once figured out that on average he publishes one item a week—and four books a year. But, then, work for Hall is neither alienated labor nor is it a function of a puritanical work ethic. It is rather an obsession and a devotion. Hall learned how he felt about it when, in a conversation with a psychoanalyst, he meant to say "life" and out came "work."

In his book *Life Work* (1993), Hall describes his methods and schedules: how he apportions his hours to a variety of writerly tasks, managing to juggle all sorts of literary balls thanks to his ability to compartmentalize, his seize-the-day morning vigor, and his discovery that he could dictate his letters and much of his prose—enough to keep several typists busy. As one who is similarly work-driven, I had to smile in recognition when I came to the passage in which Hall refers to himself as a maker of lists who, when he accomplishes something unplanned, writes the item down, "in order to feel the satisfaction of crossing it out."

The shadow of death hangs over *Life Work*. Several months into the writing of the book, Hall found out he had liver cancer. Surgery and chemotherapy followed. He lost, he writes, "two-thirds of a liver and nine-tenths of [his] complacency." The doctor gave him a one-in-three chance of living five years. That was in 1992, when Hall was sixty-four. He suddenly found it hard to complete a thought about "next" year or the year after. And it became harder still when Don's beloved wife Jane was diagnosed with leukemia last winter. As I write, Don and Jane are on the way to Seattle, where she hopes to have a bone marrow transplant. Don is a man of ferocious energy, but even he has limits; he has given up a number of responsibilities, and he has asked me to edit the Poets on Poetry series. It is an honor to take the baton. On behalf of the poets and the readers that he has served so well I want to thank Donald Hall and to rededicate this series to the principles that he has embodied in his exemplary literary career.

*October 1994*

# Part 1

# What Is It?
# The Question of Postmodernism

***What do the following have in common?***

—A poem about the characters in a book, and about the reader of that book, and about what they are doing when the book is not being read. [The poem, "Reading in Place," is in Mark Strand's collection *The Continuous Life* (1990).]

—An American television series combining the elements of a murder mystery, a soap opera, a parody of a murder mystery, and a parody of a soap opera, in which the expected generic conventions occur but ironically, everything happening as if between invisible quotation marks. [The series is *Twin Peaks* by David Lynch (1990).]

—A British television series in which a hard-boiled detective plot—long on wisecracks, tough talk, trench coats, and mean streets—is systematically punctuated by the crooning of romantic tunes from the 1940s. The incongruousness of the juxtaposition is calculated, dramatizing that the cynical detective is in fact a disillusioned romantic in the Sinatra manner. [The series is *The Singing Detective* by Dennis Potter (1986).]

—A story whose characters include the pieces on a board game as well as the people who manipulate them. What is the inner life of Colonel Mustard? Miss Scarlet? Professor Plum? [The story is "A Game of

*AWP Chronicle,* December 1994.

Clue" from Steven Millhauser's book *The Barnum Museum* (1990).]

—A book of sestinas about Perry Mason, Della Street, Paul Drake, Hamilton Burger, and Lieutenant Tragg. [The book is *The Whole Truth* by James Cummins (1986).]

—A novel about the adventures of a feline character from a once beloved, now defunct comic strip who gets to be psychoanalyzed, witnesses the development of the atomic bomb, and speaks in a punning idiolect in which "capitalism" becomes "keepitallism," psychoanalysis "sighcowandallis," nuclear physics "newclear fizzsticks," and virus "whyrus." [The novel, based on George Herriman's comic strip of the same name, is *Krazy Kat* by Jay Cantor (1988).]

—A novel about the lives of movie protagonists before and after the Hollywood films in which they figure. What happens to Rick Blaine after he and Captain Renault toast the beginning of their beautiful friendship at the end of *Casablanca*? What does George Bailey do with all the money he gets at the close of *It's a Wonderful Life*? What was Kay Corleone's childhood like, and how does she get along with her estranged son after her husband exiles her from the family in *The Godfather, Part II*? [The novel that answers these and other such questions is *Suspects* by David Thomson (1985).]

—A sestina that contains the name of a flower, a tree, a fruit, a game, and a famous old lady, as well as the word *bathtub,* in every line: "In the apple tree Queen Mary of the Chrysanthemums shared a grape rook bathtub with her insect lamp." [The poem, written collaboratively by John Ashbery and Kenneth Koch, is entitled "Crone Rhapsody" (c. 1956).]

—A poem in which the parts of speech turn into human characters springing into action: "A lonely Conjunction here and there would call, 'And! But!' / But the Adjective did not emerge." [The poem, "Permanently," is in Kenneth Koch's collection *Thank You* (1962).]

—A painting of a Dutch Masters cigar box, whose label itself reproduces a famous Rembrandt; also, paintings of the Camel cigarette label, the French hundred franc note, and the menu at the Cedar Tavern. [The paintings were all done in the fifties by Larry Rivers.]

What all these have in common is that each can be said to embody the spirit of postmodernism. The first seven are relatively recent instances; the works by Ashbery, Koch, and Rivers were ahead of the wave.

### What is postmodernism?

Nobody knows for sure, except you're supposed to say that before talking confidently about it. Best not to be too solemn. Nobody, with the exception of a few academics, really likes the term, but it won't go away, and it does afford a way to make sense of some recent developments in American fiction and poetry.

Postmodernism is best understood not as a rigid concept or a coherent ideological stance but as a bundle of shared impulses and tendencies amounting to a kind of common spirit. More than anything else, postmodernism is an attitude, and that attitude is definitively ironic. It revels in comedy and exalts the spirit of parody and play. It treats the monuments of tradition in particular with jubilant irreverence. The distinction between artifacts of high and low culture gets leveled. Characters and lives are confused. Poems based on intricate rules are written in a kind of partnership with the language, an attempt to bring out the poetry latent in the language rather than to impose meaning on language. Generic conventions—particularly those of gangster movies, detective novels, and comic strips—are cheerfully appropriated and just as cheerfully deviated from, as the author wishes. Postmodernism is the triumph of irony.

Fragments are postmodernist, as is the act of completing somebody else's unfinished work. Hoaxes by nature are postmodernist. So are pseudonyms. The Portuguese poet Pessoa, who wrote poems under many pseudonyms, each of which he outfitted with a full biography and a distinctive style, was an arch-postmodernist *avant la lettre* or—to use a phrase favored by the members of the Oulipo, the French society of mathematically inclined writers committed to the development of cunning new forms—a plagiarist by anticipation.

When Jean-Paul Belmondo in Jean-Luc Godard's *Breathless* (1959) tries to die like Humphrey Bogart in a thirties gangster movie, he is announcing the official birth of postmodernism. (Belmondo spends much of that movie posing in front of old Bogart posters.) The patron saints of postmodernism are Jorge Luis Borges and Vladimir Nabokov, writers who favor parables, labyrinths, mirror games, riddles and linguistic oddities, false-bottomed narratives, artifice conscious of itself as artifice. The paradigmatic postmodernist gesture is the one performed by Borges's Pierre Menard, who sets out to write a book called *Don Quixote* that is identical in every particular to the *Don Quixote* of Cervantes—word for word—but is nevertheless superior to that of Cervantes, because it would be harder to write the book in Argentina in the twentieth century than in Spain in the sixteenth when, presumably, the medieval chivalrous ideal was closer to hand. Repetition is postmodernism in action. Everything happens twice, "the first time as tragedy, the second time as farce": Karl Marx's famous remark about history repeating itself is obligatory in any discussion of postmodernism.

Experiments in discontinuous narration are postmodernist, as is the attempt to incorporate the texture of multiplicity into fiction. Robert Coover does both at once in his famous story "The Babysitter." He constantly interrupts his narrative, scrambling the order of events, and he provides different outcomes for the same fictional predicament. You will find the ideal of multiplicity in its purest form in a novel entitled *April March* by the Borgesian character Herbert Quain. A purely conceptual novel by a nonexistent author, *April March* branches out backwards: an event is described in Chapter 1; each of the following three chapters lays out a plausible prior event leading up to the one described in Chapter 1; for each of these three, three subsequent chapters detail prior events that could have led to it. Borges explains: "The entire work, thus, constitutes nine novels; each novel contains three long chapters. (The first chapter, naturally, is common to all.) The temper of one of these novels is symbolic; that of another, psychological; of another, communist; of still another, anti-communist; and so on."[1] It is an experiment in multiplicity and at the same time a quizzing of causality.

What isn't postmodernism? James Joyce's *Ulysses*. I have heard the postmodernist argument: that Joyce lifts his plot from an earlier work and that he deviates from a linear narrative. It is, moreover, true that *Ulysses* is thick with artifice, full of the spirit of play and the energy of parody. But the source of *Ulysses* is Homer's *Odyssey*, not a comic book. And Joyce's high literary ambition, like his heroic conception of the artist, is strikingly at variance with common postmodernist practice. Joyce's comic vision is robustly affirmative, not narrowly mocking. And then, too, the anger, passion, and humor in *Ulysses* have a moral end; even Molly Bloom's soliloquy, with its frank celebration of carnality, is moral in the sense of furthering an enlightened attitude toward human sexuality.

It sometimes vexes me to know that some people automatically associate poststructuralism with postmodernism when in fact the two events (if that's what they are) seem to me fundamentally different. Postmodernism is a question of art and attitude, poststructuralism of criticism and crisis. Poststructuralism, in the form of deconstruction, is primarily an academic phenomenon; postmodernism is not. A form of literary criticism aspiring to the condition of philosophy, poststructuralism is hopelessly mired in epistemological questions (the "what-can-we-know" impasse) and has a deliberately anti-aesthetic bias. Deconstructive readings set out to demonstrate that all texts subvert their authors' intentions, and themselves: not that the text is meaningless but that it can invariably be reduced to a pair of incompatible propositions. The result of the systematic application of this procedure is that literature is indeterminate; knowledge is inaccessible; art has the status of a TV commercial, hawking not a consumer product but an ideological purchase; and the author is dead.

In contrast to this dreary exercise, postmodernism would seem to be a glorification of the aesthetic impulse despised by deconstructionists. A deconstructionist denigrates a literary work by likening it to an advertisement. A postmodernist elevates the same advertisement (if only ironically) by treating it as an aesthetic statement. There is a big difference. Of course, some postmodernist works are better than others—some may be brilliant, others meretricious—and it is important to discriminate between them. But that is another question.

I realize that poststructuralism and postmodernism may seem, or can be made to seem, like parallel developments, differing responses to the same set of circumstances. Certainly there are areas of overlap. I have used the phrase "soft-core deconstruction" for works that artfully use deconstructive tactics or procedures without adhering to the dogmas of Jacques Derrida and Paul de Man. For example, the logical conundrum at the conclusion of Philip Roth's *Operation Shylock*, "This confession is false," is a deconstructive gesture deployed for postmodernist purposes remote from the teachings of academic deconstruction. It is, however, possible that postmodernism in art has nothing more in common with poststructuralism in criticism than the prefix *post*. Both are in a sense postdated events, conscious of the lateness of the hour.

### What time is it?

The postmodernist answer is, "Later than it's ever been." The prefix *post* announces the anxiety of belatedness—of living in the shadow of some greater event, having arrived too late to affect things. (Shelley, the poet of aftermath, names the condition when he describes "the awful shadow of some unseen power" in his great "Hymn to Intellectual Beauty." The spirit Shelley addresses is evanescent, "like memory of music fled" or like a vision that refuses to stay.) The implication of that *post* is that the present exists less in its own right than as a sequel—just as the phrase "postwar era," applied to the years 1945 to 1960, suggests a domestic sequel to World War II. The present is felt to be somehow inferior to, or less consequential than, the immediate past.

There is a simple historical explanation for this general condition: the public events and personalities of the first half of the century, in particular the period from 1914 to 1945, overshadow their counterparts since. The period in question encompassed two World Wars, the Russian Revolution, the

Great Depression, Hitler and the Nazis, Stalin and Stalinism, Mussolini and Fascism, the Spanish Civil War, the Holocaust, and the making and dropping of the atomic bomb. All you need do is compare today's world leaders—in stature, in dramatic interest, and in world historical importance—with Churchill, Roosevelt, Gandhi, et al. to become instantly aware of a great discrepancy. For people born after 1945, there is the sense that the key events defining our collective imaginations took place back then, before we were born, the sense that the events that provide the terms and touchstones of our moral beliefs and philosophical doubts date from this earlier period.

This historical inferiority complex helps to account for the mood of nostalgia that pervades the worlds of art and entertainment today.[2] The creative life of our period is haunted by that of the immediate past, as postmodernism is haunted by modernism. This gets fetishized by, for example, Roy Lichtenstein in ironic homages to Mondrian and Matisse, or by Woody Allen in movies that constantly compare themselves to earlier, more heroic treatments of the same themes. Last year's *Manhattan Murder Mystery*, for example, deliberately reminds viewers of *Double Indemnity, Rear Window, Vertigo,* and *Psycho.* In desperation some artists may affect a self-consciously original manner, but they are whistling in the dark. The governing feeling is that originality is impossible. Reality is a matter of repetition. As the popular solecism has it, "It's *déjà-vu* all over again." The poet Andrei Codrescu has summed up one major difference between modernism and postmodernism: "The Modernist command was Pound's 'Make It New.' The postmodern imperative is 'Get It Used.' "

### Why all this irony?

Because as Philip Roth observed thirty years ago, reality in the United States so far outstrips the inventive capacity of any satirist. Because in our society knowledge has tended to equal disillusionment, and any affirmation of belief must therefore be made in the very teeth of disbelief. Because the legacy of Vietnam, and the continuing saga of racial hatred and rage, made the old patriotic pieties seem as redolent of childhood as

Tinkerbell. Or because there is something fundamentally unserious about our culture. Because you can't write a love scene the same way when the divorce rate approaches 50 percent. And you can't write a well-made morality play, whose idea is that you can't be happy unless you're good, or an old-fashioned detective novel, whose moral is that crime doesn't pay, when the benefits of an insider trading scam or a crude physical attack on a competitor far outweigh the penalties.

### Where did postmodernism come from?

From architecture. While there is only a limited amount of overlap between architectural modernism and literary modernism, there is a strong sense of affinity between architectural postmodernism and literary postmodernism. Implicit in both is a strong emphasis on parody and pastiche. (One difference between these two things is that parody has a critical point to make and pastiche doesn't.) A prime example of postmodernist architecture is Philip Johnson's AT&T building in midtown Manhattan with its famous Chippendale top. The incongruity is deliberate: it is held to be a positive value to use the styles associated with different movements or periods without fear of incoherence. Literary postmodernism is similarly eclectic and inconsistent. The postmodernist author tends to blur genres, stealing from all over, conflating kinds of diction, moving from the funny pages to the classics with the speed of a distracted newspaper reader in the subway, who jumps from the budgetary standstill on Capitol Hill to the tight race in the American League East without necessarily finishing either story.

There is also such a thing as deconstructive architecture, whose apotheosis to date was a show at the Museum of Modern Art in New York City a few years ago. The objective of this movement seems to be the perpetuation of ugliness. The deconstructive architect wants to locate, and to emphasize, the contaminating flaw in an architectural structure—to show how, like a literary text scrutinized in a deconstructive seminar, it collapses from within—as if every house were a house divided against itself.

### What's hot and what's not?

In Marshall McLuhan's terms, the abstract expressionists (Jackson Pollock, Willem de Kooning, Mark Rothko, Franz Kline, et al.) were "hot" in the sense that radio as a medium is hot or that the personalities of Roosevelt and Churchill and Hitler were hot. An abstract expressionist painting was the product of great difficulty and struggle, even when that painting consisted of a single vertical stripe on a massive red canvas. The avatars of pop art, such as Andy Warhol and Robert Rauschenberg, who supplanted the abstract expressionists as the stars of the art world, were "cool" in the sense that television is cool. "You have to have time to feel sorry for yourself if you're going to be a good abstract expressionist," said Rauschenberg, for whom art meant never having to say you're sorry. As for Warhol, his soup cans and soap pads are insolently easy, nonchalant, *no sweat*. Other cool personalities of the early sixties include John F. Kennedy, James Bond, Johnny Carson, and the Project Mercury astronauts. (Among current TV talk show hosts it is clear that David Letterman has a lot more cool than Jay Leno.) Modernism in this particular sense was a hot phenomenon; postmodernism, a cool one. William Butler Yeats: very hot. Robert Lowell: hot. John Ashbery: cool as a cucumber.

The best way to capture McLuhan's sense of *hot* and *cool* is to compare a radio announcer's play-by-play account of a baseball game (hot) with an airy TV commentator's take on the same action (cool). Radio requires the listener's imaginative involvement; TV turns the viewer into a passive spectator. Only in the movies does a mad TV newscaster incite people to open their windows and scream their frustrations out into the street.

### What is the relation of postmodernism to television and the movies?

Postmodernism is equally the product of disillusionment and of its opposite, the enchantment of illusions. The disillusionment is expressed through irony. The enchantment is celebrated through the movies—through cinematic metaphors and images, narrative devices associated with the movies, or references to specific films.

Film is hot. Videotape is cool. In contrast with the movies, which are associated with the glamour of nostalgia, television is identified with the present, with childhood and adolescence, and with mediocrity—a mediocrity so perfect you'd think that TV producers and directors had consciously set their sights on it.

Because television dominates the living room there is the strong sense that our reality, our public reality, is mediated: we know that the "news" is not what happens but what is reported by "the media." "Yet it is all offered as 'today's news,' as if we somehow had a right to it, as though it were a part of our lives / That we'd be silly to refuse. Here, have another— crime or revolution? Take your pick." These lines from John Ashbery's long poem "The Skaters" (in *Rivers and Mountains,* 1966) imply that one way of dealing with the "news" is to refuse it. A determined effort to ignore the news or to include current events with a kind of neutral conviviality is a mark of the New York School. Frank O'Hara began one of his "I do this I do that" poems with the excited line, "Khrushchev is coming on the right day!" In the poem Khrushchev symbolizes nothing, stands for nothing, is merely part of the mental landscape, the name in a headline one September day in 1959; the real subject of the poem is unexpectedly traditional: the wind ("New York seems blinding and my tie is blowing up the street / I wish it would blow off") of inspiration.

The "news" enters recent American fiction in a twisted form: where plot was, conspiracy shall be. A sense of perplexity about what is real goes together with a fascination with what is fake, simulated, spurious, constructed. A couple of years ago I read a news story about a man who manufactured replicas of the Maltese Falcon—a fake of a fake, since the supposedly priceless, gem-encrusted piece of black avian statuary in both Dashiell Hammett's novel and John Huston's movie is a fake. The man's mail-order business was thriving.

It is possible that reality never existed in unmediated form. But it is certainly the case that never before have so many people held the conviction that this is so. The emphasis shifts from the *what* to the *how* of any statement: the means and medium of communication, the telling as opposed to the tale. This was announced with deadly accuracy by McLuhan thirty years ago.

But television's flattening of reality goes further. There is this paradox: nothing is real except what's on television, yet television makes everything unreal. In addition to turning viewers into laid-back voyeurs, television affords the most advanced technological means to divorce image from substance. Paranoia, a reasonable response, becomes the characteristic mental condition of both the reader and the characters in postmodernist fiction. Since TV culture is the culture of the commercial and the paid political advertisement, there is always the lingering suspicion that what you see on the news was paid for, inauthentic, cooked up by some media specialist employed to fool some of the people all the time. It is not an accident that paranoia is a favorite postmodernist predicament: you get a strong dose of it in the novels of Don de Lillo and Thomas Pynchon and in the science fiction of Philip K. Dick.

An outstanding TV skit from the eighties shows a comic impersonator of Ronald Reagan bumbling amiably outside the White House, befuddled and out of touch—but once the reporters have left and he is safely behind closed doors, we see him clearly on top of the situation, giving orders, in complete control, a veritable tiger. In an age of irony, paranoia can have a comic edge. On the other hand, there was that memorable moment in 1983 when the editors of *Newsweek* decided to put the so-called Hitler diaries on the cover of the magazine. The hoax had not yet been exposed, but the writer of the cover story was taking no chances. Just in case his bosses had been conned, he wrote a perfect *Newsweek* sentence declaring that "it almost doesn't matter in the end" whether the diaries (for which the magazine had paid a great deal of money) turn out to be real or fake. There you have it in a nutshell, postmodernist paranoia: no way to distinguish truth from simulacrum, and in the end, someone reliably to say that it doesn't matter.

Television gave us white noise. In trailer parks, in motels, in apartments, in the lounge areas of college dormitories, in fitness centers and bars and public spaces of all kinds, the television is always on in the background, invading the place, heard though not listened to. It is only fair that the space of the postmodernist novel should be similarly invaded by secondhand language: canned laughter, the manic huckster's voice, the voice on the tape of a recorded telephone message, the memorized speech of the airplane flight attendant, and so forth. A good idea for a postmodernist story: a tale told exclusively through white noise and secondhand language.

The most powerful episode in Oliver Stone's movie *Natural Born Killers* (1994) is that of the girl molested by her father, which Stone presents as if it were a situation comedy, laugh track and all. The incongruity produces a fine disturbance; in effect, Stone shows us what the paradigmatic TV family sitcom is busy repressing. That is one manifestation of the postmodernist attitude toward television. A more joyous one informs David Trinidad's poem "Reruns," which consists of seventeen haiku, each of which strictly observes the haiku's syllabic requirements, about television programs from the sixties.

Postmodernism and feminism seem to have converged in the figure of the Barbie doll. Barbie is the subject of a book by M. G. Lord (*Forever Barbie*, 1994) and of a virtual mini-genre of poems, including "Barbie's Ferrari" by Lynne McMahon and an entire sequence entitled *It's My Body* by Denise Duhamel.

Postmodernist hell is a comic nightmare: to be trapped inside the television, bouncing between channels, from quiz show to horse opera, as happens to Mr. and Mrs. Couch Potato in the comedy film *Stay Tuned*.

***Does the postmodernist obsession with two-dimensionality—as if our reality lacked a dimension—come from a steady diet of television?***

No, from comic books. Even before Roy Lichtenstein's "true romance" paintings of the early sixties, with their clinching couples and thought bubbles, bright colors and Benday dots, comic strips provided infectious imagery. Cartoon characters, escaping from the cartoonist's sketch pad, are featured in big-budget Hollywood films (*Superman, Batman, Dick Tracy*), but they also turn up regularly in highbrow writing. John Ashbery has a poem chronicling the adventures of "Daffy Duck in Hollywood." Art Spiegelman has won major book prizes for his two-volume comic book *Maus,* about his parents' experience of the Holocaust, in which the Jews are mice and the Nazis cats; Spiegelman doesn't diminish the gravity of his narrative, he just translates it into a demotic idiom. Steven Millhauser has a story called "Klassik Komix #1," which renders T. S. Eliot's "The Love Song of J. Alfred Prufrock" as if it were a comic book, with a paragraph of prose devoted to each panel. Nearly all of panel thirty-nine is taken up by a gigantic orange and red fruit against a black background: "The fruit has eyes and two thick black frowning eyebrows. In the lower left-hand-corner a tiny Alfred looks up at the fruit in alarm. In the thought balloon beside his head are the words: DO I DARE TO EAT A PEACH?"

Millhauser's story appeared in *The Barnum Museum* (1990). A few months after that book appeared in print, a freelance English cartoonist named Martin Rowson published *The Waste Land* in the form of a comic book. Translating Eliot's poem into comic-book imagery, Rowson added a hard-boiled detective idiom; in effect, he showed *The Waste Land* through the lens of *The Maltese Falcon* and *The Big Sleep.* The Holy Grail becomes the Maltese Falcon, the figure of Tiresias is a drag queen, and the writing is full of sarcastic similes that are just slightly off: "At dusk the buzzards started screaming like a mother whose son has blown the week's drinking money on college fees."

### Who put the mustache on the Mona Lisa?

We live not in an era when a painter put a mustache on the Mona Lisa but in an era when that famous gesture became a cliché—a time when such "shocks" are routine. "But today there is no point in looking to imaginative new methods / Since all of them are in constant use," wrote John Ashbery in "Definition of Blue" (in *The Double Dream of Spring,* 1970). Today the spirit of irony and parody must involve our own sacred objects. That is one of the brilliant strokes in Kenneth Koch's book *One Thousand Avant-Garde Plays* (1988). The 112 short plays in the book exemplify the avant-garde impulse and mock it at the same time. There is an aura of cultural sexiness about being "avant-garde," though the term itself remains as slippery as ever. You can't define it, but you can demonstrate its possibilities over and over—and that is Koch's mandate. Koch proposes, for example, six ways of turning Hamlet's "To be or not to be" soliloquy into an exemplary act of avant-garde theater; he presents the same speech with six different sets of stage directions. In one case, the hero interrupts himself after the "sea of troubles" sentence—he lights a cigarette, inhales, exhales, and walks offstage ("Smoking Hamlet"). In another, two actors go through the motions of the Little Red Riding Hood fairy tale while reciting Hamlet's speech ("Little Red Riding Hamlet"). In a third, a team of readers recites the speech one syllable at a time, changing their posture after every six syllables ("Team Hamlet"). The irreverence is not in regard to Hamlet but in regard to the avant-garde ideal that is seemingly embodied in these miniature verse dramas. My favorite is "After the Return of the Avant-Garde," which ends with this exchange: "Which is more avant-garde—a giraffe or an elephant?" "A giraffe is more avant-garde, but an elephant is more surreal."

### What accounts for the popularity of the sestina in this postmodernist era?

It is an article of the postmodernist faith that language has a mind and a will of its own, an autonomous existence full of meaning and mystery. Unwilling to wait for lightning to strike, the poet manufactures inspiration by linguistic invention—by playing with words rather than by trying to exercise mastery and control over them. Writing a sestina is an excellent example. A word game tricked out as a mathematical structure, or vice versa, the sestina consists of thirty-nine lines distributed over six six-line stanzas and a final triplet; six words, occurring in a prescribed order, conclude all thirty-nine lines of the poem. Writing a sestina is, as John Ashbery has noted, "like riding a bicycle downhill and having the pedals push your feet." The benefit for the poet is that he or she may wind up in territory not usually visited. The poet has to spend so much time solving the formal puzzle—how to get the six end-words (or *teleutons*) to occur and recur in the exact order required—that there is little time left to worry about the coherence of the imagery or the logic of the argument. The censorious ego, being otherwise occupied, steps aside and lets the poet's unconscious shoot directly onto the page. That is one important reason this medieval form is more popular in the English-speaking world today than anywhere ever before.

### Where will it end?

A postmodernist trick is to pull the rug out from under the reader. The speaker at the close of his presentation, sneaking a look at his wristwatch, smiles enigmatically and says, "What I've just said isn't true." I am tempted to do something like that. To say that postmodernism, so useful in giving academics something to talk about, is a fiction. To argue that we are not *post-anything*. We are, miserably or splendidly, ourselves, living now, living here. What I've been calling postmodernism is really an extension of modernism, not a repudiation of it. "Postmodernism is a misnomer," writes Janet Malcolm. "The architects and urban planners laboring under its rubric haven't abandoned modernism but have continued to work serenely in its idiom." You could make the same argument with regard to art and literature. It could be that nothing in postmodernism is new: all the tendencies of postmodernism were already there, if only embryonically, in modernism. Even the tendency to pull the rug out from under the reader goes back to modernist works by Henry James and Joseph Conrad.

Well, maybe. But when I look at my own enduring critical preoccupations—my fascination with hoaxes and fragments, with the poets of the New York School and their painterly pals, with hard-boiled murder mysteries and forties flicks, with parodies and paranoia—I know they suggest so strong an affinity with the postmodernist spirit that to deny it as a potent force could only seem disingenuous. The real question, as I see it, is whether postmodernism is as innocent as it sometimes looks. I would like to think that the devices, the attitude and tone of postmodernism can be used—and used with a vengeance—for moral as well as aesthetic ends. Susan Sontag in her essay on "Camp" said that the artistic temper of our century is composed of homosexual aestheticism and Jewish moral earnestness in concert. That is well said. It remains a challenge to try to bring these forces together in some way that preserves their individual functions and transcends them in the lasting form of art.

## NOTES

1. The result is (or would be) a single volume containing seven chapters out of which the reader is invited to construct nine separate novels.

2. Consider the Broadway musical. In March 1994, the following musicals were playing on Broadway: From the sixties, *She Loves Me;* from the fifties, *My Fair Lady, Guys and Dolls,* and *Damn Yankees;* from the forties, *Carousel;* and from the thirties, *Crazy for You.* The much ballyhooed Toronto production of *Showboat* arrived in October 1994.

# Part 2

# Poetry and Fiction

# Blank (Verse) Generation

The corpse of poetry is, if you will, a dead metaphor. The force of repetition has turned the demise of verse into a truism. But in dark corners of Manhattan, late at night, far from the eye of English-department undertakers, the corpse has been stirring. The heart of the revenant form is a big, dark, brick-walled loft on Third Street and Avenue C called the Nuyorican Poets' Café. Verbal violence occurs there every Friday night in the form of competitive readings called "slams." Winning poets earn the right to advance toward the Grand Slam the next month.

The poetry of the Nuyorican and other such venues is a Clinton-era form, though the Nuyorican predates the new Administration. It is democratic, multicultural, a species of nightclub infotainment related to the new-age confessionals of Robert Bly's men's movement and the twelve-step program. It finds its sources in rap, *The Simpsons,* Jack Kerouac, Walt Whitman. It is often earnest, sometimes funny, sometimes ribald, always loud. It has the vitality of vulgarity.

All sorts of bohemians and would-be bohemians have attached themselves to the revival, which actually originated in Los Angeles a few years ago. Tuli Kupferberg, former lead singer of the mid-sixties' post-beat rock band the Fugs, is back on the East Village scene reading his poems. Romeo Gigli, the neo-romantic fashion designer, has hosted public poetry readings at his store on East Sixty-ninth Street. Famously awful poetry readings are held at Coffee Shop, the supertrendy haircut hangout on Union Square West. At

---

*New York Observer,* March 29, 1993.

Jackie 60, an itinerant nightclub featuring transvestites and downtown relics like Michael Musto, poets declaim from an (unplugged) electric chair. Poets, or people describing themselves thus, have infiltrated such formerly verseless places as No Bar on East Ninth Street, where on a recent Tuesday the self-proclaimed "Pussy Poets" held forth on the age-old question of whether feminism and makeup are compatible. Maya Angelou legitimized the new multicultural dispensation by reading her eight-minute-long ode to democratic egalitarianism at President Clinton's inauguration.

Perhaps the most notorious and lucrative poem of the nineties is a work entitled "What Fits?" Composed by Max Blagg, a forty-three-year-old British-born New Yorker, these truly terrible verses in praise of dungarees—"that fit like a glove / like an old lover coming back for more"—were written for and featured in a TV commercial for The Gap. Mr. Blagg earned enough through residuals from this ad (it went off the air in December after an eight-month run) to quit his bartending job in SoHo and devote himself full time to poetry. Soon, no doubt, even *New York* magazine will lionize the new breed of upstart poets under the headline "The New Bohemians" or some such.[1]

On a recent Friday night at the Nuyorican, I caught the following acts. Mike Ladd, a student at hip Hampshire College in Amherst, Massachusetts, rapped his poem with rat-tat-tat rapidity: "I'm a nigger with a surfboard riding the wave of Armageddon." His couplets were topical: "Madonna thinks she's black / Santa Claus is on crack." Jane Goldberg, introduced as "one of the queens of the tap-rap scene," danced and sang a lyric to the tune of "Tea for Two." The lyric was about swallowing sperm, "sushi-flavored sperm ice cream," to be more specific.

Some of the poets didn't fare so well. The author and presenter of "Demon Dance," one Vernon Frazier, feverishly

---

1. About six weeks after this article was published, *New York* ran a cover story on poetry slams under the headline "The Beats Are Back."

played the string bass while chanting a poem about ego loss and selflessness with great self-absorption. The audience heckled him mercilessly: "Get rid of him!" "Next!"

Many of the poems were as perishable as the sayings on teabag tags or as meretricious as the text-heavy agitprop on the walls of the Whitney Biennial. All too typical was the poet with the punk haircut who went from why to plaintive why: "Why must men be in the word that describes my gender?" "Why do men rape us?"

All of this can be amusing. As to whether it qualifies as poetry . . . the jury is still out. But that may not be the important question. Much of what I heard at the Nuyorican seemed to belong in a new and different category altogether, a hybrid of performance art and TV shtick, a sort of self-consciously outrageous multicultural variety show.

At my table one night were two clean-cut first-year students at the School of Visual Arts, commuters from Long Island and Brooklyn. It was clear from their rapt expressions that they felt themselves to be at the very core of lower Manhattan hipdom. It was also clear that they knew next to nothing about poetry as it had been practiced up to that point. One of them said that his favorite poet was the singer Tom Waits.

The traditional poetry world tends to look askance at the whole downtown phenomenon. "It's bogus, an exercise in crudity," said a poet friend. "It rewards people who yell the loudest and curse the hardest. That's not an atmosphere conducive to real poetry." "Anything that brings attention and energy to poetry is a wonderful thing," said William Wadsworth, executive director of the Academy of American Poets. "On the other hand, my strong feeling is that a lot of the actual poetry is more performance oriented, and even, in some instances, more like stand-up comedy than poetry. Real poetry has more to do with thought and reflection." Still, Mr. Wadsworth's organization will soon participate in a Friday event at the Nuyorican.[2] And

2. This turned out to be a "poetry game show" pitting teams from Poets House, the Academy of American Poets, Teachers and Writers Collaborative, and Poets & Writers. The contests included a

according to Jeanne McCulloch, an editor of the *Paris Review,* the literary journal and the poets of the Nuyorican have a standing challenge to a slam.

Robert Polito, director of the writing program at the New School for Social Research, supplied context while withholding approval: "Poetry slams carry to a logical extreme the emphasis on poetry readings in the last twenty years. Many poets now write poems with an eye to how they will be performed at readings. That hasn't always been good for the poets concerned."

Unlike many of the critics of poetry slams, though, Mr. Polito has actually been to the Nuyorican, and he liked what he heard well enough to enlist Bob Holman, the café's guiding spirit, to teach two courses at the New School next fall, one on performance poetry and one on the New York Poetry Slam experience. I met Mr. Holman at the Nuyorican café one Friday. Forty-five, wearing a leather porkpie hat, the scraggly, bearded, round-faced impresario describes himself as both a "poetry addict" and a "poetry activist," committed to the task of widening the audience for poetry at whatever cost. "No one would think to say, 'I don't like music,'" he said. "Yet people say, 'I don't like poetry' all the time."

During the early eighties, Mr. Holman headed the Poetry Project at St. Mark's Church, then the trendsetter in hip New York poetry events. "I had spent many years in the trenches writing press releases, which was like sending paper airplanes into the void. And I came to the conclusion that it's hard to change the world without being a part of it."

With the poetry slam Mr. Holman thinks he has pretty much figured out a way to assure poetry's survival in an age dominated by louder, brassier media. "Poetry," he said, "is undergoing a fundamental change through rap and a revival of the oral tradition."

What Joel Grey was to *Cabaret,* Mr. Holman is to the poetry slam. He maintains a ceaseless stream of clever patter, some-

---

Dead Poets' Slam and a Poetry Spelling Bee. I served as quizmaster as Mr. Wadsworth's squad triumphed at "What's That Line?"

times twitting the audience, sometimes spoofing the proceedings, darting rapidly from instant epigrams ("There is no poem unless there is a heckler standing by to spike it into existence") to high art (he declaimed the last stanza of William Butler Yeats's "Easter 1916" the week after the bombing of the World Trade Center). The audience, mostly college students but with a smattering of slumming uptown literati, lapped it up.

Talking to Mr. Holman, I soon discovered that he and I had been classmates at Columbia College, circa 1968. At Columbia, Mr. Holman discovered sex, drugs, rock 'n' roll, radical politics, and the mischievous poetic consciousness of Kenneth Koch, who became a profound influence. We both took Koch's modern poetry class that year, a year of maximum tumult on the Columbia campus, with students occupying five buildings to protest the building of a gym in Morningside Heights. "Remember the time Koch read some lines of Whitman and then hugged himself saying, 'Oh, Walt, I love you'? I'd never seen a poet having that intimate a relationship to poetry before. I've been a real politicized beast ever since Columbia, and a prankster since reading the Dadaists and surrealists."

After rapper Mike Ladd's machine-gun recital of his poem "The Tear Refinery," Mr. Holman wrapped himself around the microphone, leading the applause. Then he congratulated the poet for his "conceit of the industrialization of the emotions," instructed one of his Nuyorican co-directors to "add that to the image list," and intoned gleefully, "now we take that thing of beauty and treat it like a bar code. The one rule in a poetry slam is that the best poet always loses."

At a typical Nuyorican slam, judges—who are usually pulled from the audience and have no special qualifications—rate the contestants on a scale from one to ten in a decimal-happy system designed to parody the scoring of Olympic gymnastics. For instance, a wretched poem about Morgan Fairchild in jail pulled in scores of 6.7, 8.2, 8.0, 7.5, and 7.7. "We had a poem here one night that was rated minus infinity," Mr. Holman told the crowd. "Zero is for a poem whose words should be eaten, not read. Ten causes orgasm."

Ties are broken with an instant haiku sudden death over-time round—the poets have to improvise on the spot. The winner gets ten dollars, the loser five, with the audience counting out the bills one by one.

The obvious antecedents of the current breed of poets are the Beats. In the fifties, the favored props for poetry readings were sunglasses, bongo drums, and saxophones. More recently, at the Naropa Institute's Jack Kerouac School of Disembodied Poetics in Boulder, Colorado, in the early eighties, aging Beat bard Gregory Corso handed out water pistols at readings and encouraged the audience to squirt the poet at the sound of a bad line or trite phrase.

A poet named Marc Smith is usually credited with inventing the poetry slam at the Green Mill Lounge on Chicago's North Side back in 1986, three years before Mr. Holman and his partners reopened the Nuyorican as a poets' café. (An earlier incarnation of the Nuyorican, without poetry, closed in 1982.)

But the archetype of the slam can be found in Greek mythology, in the story of Apollo's competition with Marsyas the satyr. In his wanderings, Marsyas stumbled upon a flute that the goddess Athena had discarded, since she could not play it without looking ridiculous and she hated being laughed at. Marsyas made such beautiful music with his magic flute that he bewitched the peasantry. This angered Apollo, and he challenged the satyr to an artistic duel. Marsyas should have known better than to compete with a god. Apollo was able to play his instrument, the lyre, and sing at the same time, joining words and music in a clearly superior form. The muses were the jury. It was understood that the winner could inflict the punishment of his choice on the loser. Unfortunately for Marsyas, that meant getting flayed alive.

That, actually, sounds quite a bit like a slam. The impulse to inflict physical punishment on the person of a sensitive, soul-baring poet is as old as the art itself, though for the most part it has been sublimated. Even at the most refined of readings, a preening narcissist's incessant prattle makes one's fingers move, involuntarily, toward one's pockets, in search of a tomato or an egg. As the reader limns his tenderest feelings, the minds of the audience are often consumed with Stephen King visions of torture. One way of looking at the Nuyorican and its ilk is that they bring those emotions out into the open, which psychiatrists tell us is healthy.

It goes without saying that the new scene has major limitations of its own. Thinking cannot be done with a ghetto blaster in your ear. The new poetry audience, weaned on rock and rap, tends to reward poems coming out of that tradition, as well as poems with a laugh track and erotic gurgles in them. Slams license a crowd's rabid yahooism. Even the Nuyorican has boundaries, however; when a poet in the midst of an incoherent rant took out his penis and burnt it with a lit cigarette, he was escorted out.

"A slam is an impossible event, an absolute contradiction," Mr. Holman told me with dadaist fervor when I visited him at the West Twelfth Street town house where he lives with his wife, the painter Elizabeth Murray, and their two daughters. "Rating poetry is the antithesis of what poetry is about. Having poets up there in a gladiator-style event is absurd, and that's why it's so much fun to do it. This is a form that lets poetry exist—that lets people go to a reading without thinking they're going to a reading."

When I asked Mr. Holman whether he thought of himself as an impresario, he said he liked the word because it is one that is associated with Diaghilev.

"And Ed Sullivan," I said, inadvertently hitting the jackpot. While he was a student at Columbia, Mr. Holman worked as a sing-along waiter at Your Father's Mustache, a Greenwich Village restaurant, and moonlighted by warming up audiences for *The Ed Sullivan Show*. Once, when an act didn't show up, he performed on the show itself. So Ed Sullivan, more than Kenneth Koch or Walt Whitman, may be the spiritual father of the poetry slam.

I went to the Nuyorican on the night of the infamous hecklers' slam in which the heckles, rather than the poems, are rated by the judges. For the sake of this article, I agreed to get up and read one of my own poems. I began to get second thoughts while listening to a poet named Edwin Torres read an ode to Amy Fisher in which "Camille Paglia" rhymed with "genitalia." The heckles *that* elicited were "Turn him off"; "Move—get off the fucking stage"; "Is there more?"; and "Don't you read anything but the *Post*?"

But when the moment came I dutifully got up to read my poem "The Choice." Here are some of the things that were shouted at me: "That's the strangest wet dream I ever heard"; "There's nothing like tenure"; "Is this John Updike—or Woody Allen?"; "Read someone else's poem"; and, most woundingly, "Bring back Buttafuoco."

It was worse than I had imagined. I was able to console myself, though, with the thought that this was hardly my ideal audience. And I had the classic journalist's defense mechanism: Go ahead, act like assholes, I thought, it'll make great copy.

# Our Poetic Grandparents

By seemingly universal consent, John Hollander was the perfect choice to edit the Library of America's two-volume anthology of nineteenth-century American poetry, which has become one of this season's highbrow literary hits. Hollander, whose ardor for the art is matched only by his intimidating erudition, has been having a great year. A few months ago he published his latest collection of poems, *Tesserae,* a triumph of lyric mastery and formal virtuosity.

The critical acclaim the Hollander anthology is receiving is really quite extraordinary when you consider that the field of nineteenth-century American poetry is, like the university itself, an example of what embattled professors call "a contested site of knowledge production." The battle over control of the "canon" (a sanctimonious term for "required reading") is not just an academic power struggle but an attempt to challenge the very idea of greatness—an idea at the heart of any anthology that aspires to be definitive of its period. Moreover, the insurrectionary wish to alter our sense of received literary tradition has brought about a counterinsurgency of conservators, and it would seem difficult to please both sides at once. Yet that is what Hollander has managed to do.

Capacious, comprehensive, wide ranging, and judiciously fair, the Library of America anthology presents the great body of American poetry in the century of the Louisiana Purchase, the Alamo, the Civil War, the expansion of the Western frontier, the gilded age, and the age of innocence. All the major

A review of *American Poetry: The Nineteenth Century,* ed. John Hollander. *Washington Post Book World,* December 26, 1993.

figures and minor prophets are represented, in proportions both ample and calculated to reflect degrees of greatness. (Walt Whitman gets the most pages, 220; Emily Dickinson has the longest list of titles.) At the same time the anthology offers a generous sampling of folk songs ("A Home on the Range," "Michael Row the Boat Ashore"), spirituals ("Sometimes I Feel Like a Motherless Child"), and nineteenth-century versions of American Indian poetry.

The American heritage—made up in equal parts of history, local legend, and national myth—rests in the verse monuments perpetuated in these pages. The big guns and great war horses are all here—from "the midnight ride of Paul Revere" (Longfellow's telling) to "John Brown's Body" echoing in the battlefields of the Civil War ("John Brown died that the slave might be free, / But his soul goes marching on"). Here is Ralph Waldo Emerson's tribute to the New England farmers who "fired the shot heard round the world," and here is Emma Lazarus's "New Colossus" in New York harbor welcoming Europe's "huddled masses yearning to breathe free."

Here, too, is "Old Ironsides," penned by Oliver Wendell Holmes (the jurist's father) at the age of twenty-one in 1830. The greatly popular poem saved the venerable ship, which the Navy had planned to scrap despite its heroics in the War of 1812. And here is newspaperman Ernest Lawrence Thayer's claim to fame. On June 3, 1888, Thayer devoted his pseudonymous column in the *San Francisco Examiner* to "A Ballad of the Republic," as he termed it, telling of the misery in Mudville when mighty Casey struck out in the bottom of the ninth, stranding runners on second and third: our national pastime's national poem, "Casey at the Bat."

Readers may compare Francis Scott Key's "Defence of Fort McHenry" (better known as "The Star-Spangled Banner") with Katharine Lee Bates's "America the Beautiful," which some people would rather have as our national anthem. It is a pleasantly jarring experience to see songs known by heart arranged on the page as poems, and it is valuable to have the complete text of each. (Both poems consist of four stanzas, of which only one is commonly sung.) In my mind there is no contest between them. As a hymn of thanks for god's grace and bounty, "America the Beautiful" would be an ideal song for Thanksgiving, if each national holiday had an official song. But "The Star-Spangled Banner," centering on the image of the flag and climaxing with its grand question, is the greater anthem.

Consider another pairing—this time an unlikely one. Julia Ward Howe's "Battle-Hymn of the Republic" memorializes "the grapes of wrath" and sings of "the glory of the coming of the Lord." Edgar Allan Poe's poem "To Helen" salutes "the glory that was Greece, / And the grandeur that was Rome." Nineteenth-century American poetry is in some sense the outcome of a quarrel between the traditions represented by these two poems: the one homespun, full of biblical fire, world transcendence, and a militant sense of manifest destiny; the other looking eastward to Europe, the classic Mediterranean, the mother tongue of England.

Then there is this third pregnant pairing: Walt Whitman and Emily Dickinson, the expansive Brooklyn bard ("I too lived, Brooklyn of ample hills was mine, / I too walk'd the streets of Manhattan island, and bathed in the waters around it") paired with the reclusive Amherst spinster ("A Prison gets to be a friend— / Between its Ponderous face / And Ours—a Kinsmanship express— / And in its narrow Eyes—"). As the twentieth century comes to an end, it seems increasingly clear that Dickinson and Whitman were our grandparents, the father and mother of modern American poetry, a truly odd couple. They were not social poets but celebrants of the self in communion with the universe; extremists of the imagination, solitary, exceptional, eccentric. Dickinson's poems, with their peculiar punctuation (reproduced faithfully in the Library of America anthology), are capable of taking the top of your head off, to cite her own definition of a good poem. As for Whitman, to this day I cannot tearlessly read "Crossing Brooklyn Ferry" or "When Lilacs Last in the Dooryard Bloom'd."

Many are the pleasures of rereading and reassessing that this anthology affords. "Thanatopsis," William Cullen Bryant's blank-verse meditation on death and nature, death as a part of nature, would seem to be the first major statement of the American romance. The Poe selections prove Poe to be critic-proof. Though academic critics have long patronized him, there is no denying the power of Poe's strangely musical lines and violently gothic imagination; his eternally negating raven, his fairy kingdom by the sea, are beyond rationality, so perhaps it is only natural that they cannot be explained by reason. Longfellow and Whittier, once venerated, now neglected, are both far better than your fading memory of high school English. Read Longfellow's "The Jewish Cemetery at Newport" and Whittier's "Snow-Bound" and see if you aren't moved.

Among nineteenth-century poets who deserve wider recognition, I do not know which to prefer: the visionary gleam of Jones Very, the turn-of-the-century sophistication of Trumbull Stickney, or the bitter ironies of Stephen Crane. All three are wonderful, and there are other discoveries to be made. But I would conclude this necessarily brief overview with a few words in praise of the sage of Concord, who stood in relation to Whitman's "Song of Myself" as Moses on the mountain stood in relation to the promised land.

Reading Emerson in any quantity, you are struck by how many of his poems prefigure the stances of modern poets. You can trace back to his "Fable"—which begins, "The mountain and the squirrel / Had a quarrel"—the origin of A. R. Ammons's talk-back-to-nature poems. Emerson's greatness rests in his imagination of an imperial self in a free country. Freedom is the element in which love may live, and "Give All to Love" pictures the liberation of women from obsolete attitudes and archaic practice. This is how the poem ends:

> Cling with life to the maid;
> But when the surprise,
> First vague shadow of surmise
> Flits across her bosom young
> Of a joy apart from thee,
> Free be she, fancy-free;
> Nor thou detain her vesture's hem,
> Nor the palest rose she flung

From her summer diadem.
Though thou loved her as thyself,
As a self of purer clay,
Though her parting dims the day,
Stealing grace from all alive;
Heartily know,
When half-gods go,
The gods arrive.

# Interrupted Visions

Jorie Graham may possess the most flamboyantly distinctive style of any poet of her generation. The lining and spacing in her poems are deliberately irregular, and she makes little effort to comply with other familiar conventions. Some poems break off in the middle of a thought, with a dash instead of a period, and in strategic places she will substitute a blank for a word. But the surface of a Graham poem is not just flash. The frequent dashes and italics and stammering repetitions are meant to revitalize dead language or to prevent the reader's complacency; they contribute to the fresh romantic intensity that is the outstanding feature of Graham's new book, *Region of Unlikeness*.

Graham is a poet of the interrupted vision, the story that needs to be told but somehow doesn't get told, because reality takes place in the interruptions. The idiosyncracies of her style can be understood as a way of contriving a set of formal operating procedures out of the interruptions, hesitations, repetitions, and white noise that make up the music of our daily discourse.

A study could profitably be done on Graham's unique brand of poetic closure. Her endings avoid the feeling or the look of closure; they seem to hang in the air moodily or menacingly, like unanswered questions. In fact her favorite mode is the interrogative, though she can obtain the effect without a question mark. Consider the last lines of several poems in

A review of *Region of Unlikeness,* by Jorie Graham; *The Burnt Pages,* by John Ash; *Fate,* by Ai; and *Verses Dark and Silent,* by Tom Disch. From the *Chicago Tribune,* January 1992.

*Region of Unlikeness.* "Fission" ends in the urgency of a spoken command ("Don't move, don't / wreck the shroud, don't move—"), and so does "The Hiding Place" ("*no*—tell them *no*—"), while the strong religious element in Graham's poetry asserts itself in the questions at the close of "Untitled" ("*bend down bend down O wretched wife, / do you not recognize your love?*") and "At the Cabaret *Now*":

> Tell me,
> why did we live, lord?
> Blood in a wind,
> why were we meant to live?

For a poet famous for the apparent difficulty of her work, Graham is capable of shocking directness at a pitch of controlled hysteria. This is the ultimate question in "Manifest Destiny": "Oh, why are you here on this earth, you—*you*—swarming, swirling, / carrying valises, standing on line, / ready to change your name if need be—?"

While it is clear that John Ashbery is the primary influence on Jorie Graham's conception of the poem, her work differs dramatically from his in tone and texture and feeling. An Ashbery poem may take the form of an imaginative rethinking of what an argument can be. By contrast, a Jorie Graham poem is more likely to be an experiment in nonnarrative storytelling, or what she calls "the dream called storyline." The best poems in *Region of Unlikeness* are those that grapple with history and "The Phase After History." "Fission" is set in a movie theater on the day John F. Kennedy was assassinated, "The Hiding Place" in Paris during the upheaval of 1968. "History" itself is like a mysterious equation with more than two unknowns, starting with a mythic "god x" and ending with Love: "And if she's naked now, then what is there to take off / next? / and then what will Love do?"

It helps indicate the vitality and the variousness of John Ashbery's influence that he is correctly cited as the major influence on poets of a common excellence who are otherwise as unlike one another as Jorie Graham and the British-born John Ash.

Ash has lived in New York City for the last six years and shows few signs of homesickness for his native Manchester—luckily, for he is the best thing that has happened to the "New York School" in some time. The echo of the names John Ash and John Ashbery has naturally occasioned comment, and I'm told that some poetry reading impresario has had the wit to pair Ash with the poet Wendell Berry on the same program.

*The Burnt Pages,* Ash's new book, meets the question of poetic influence head on. Ash's poem "The Ungrateful Citizens" can be read as a homage to Ashbery's "The Instruction Manual" in an exhibit meant to illustrate "the insouciance of influence." Like its predecessor, "The Ungrateful Citizens" proposes the make-believe journey as the perfect metaphor for the imagination and its project of redeeming the particulars of daily, grubby metropolitan life. Ash's mental traveler reaches a fictitious Naples, and it is paradise, described in loving detail: "even shy lovers may find corners in which to commune unnoticed / except by some musician, who wishes only to urge their love forward / from a tactful distance." But the vision cannot last; there comes the revelation that "all but the richest and most conservative citizens cannot wait to leave my Naples" and then beggars in rags materialize and declare it to be not Naples at all but "a place on which the world has turned its back." The poem is a parable about the power of the imagination—and its limits—which is Ash's great theme.

Ash has a way of making poetic capital out of his last name. It adds a dimension to "Smoke" if we take into account the name of the author:

> It is cold there and lonely,
> and the sky is a burnt page. Stay—
>
> you and you others. If we are not to become
> a dispersed people of smoke,
> the monument that is us must be built soon.

Ash's "Cigarettes" meditates on the curious fact that "fag" means homosexual in America and cigarette in England, and manages to be both merry and poignant as it solves this word-puzzle, turning an odd juxtaposition into a fine metaphysical conceit: "A cigarette is like a passion in that it is inhaled deeply / and seems to fill all the empty spaces of the body, / until, of course, it burns down, and is put out amid / the shells of pistachio nuts, or whatever trash / may be at hand, and the passion may leave traces / that in time will grow malignant."

Ash's proper element is the region of enchantment to which the imagination gives access. The whimsy in his work, the humor and wit, make it so fresh and enjoyable that the reader may not always notice right away how serious are Ash's subjects and his treatment of them. The chatty discursive lines of "Revising the Atlas"—the title another metaphor for what the imagination can and cannot do—are animated by their anxieties: "Life today is so exciting / since we are daily menaced by the prospect of extinction / in a variety of novel forms." The most moving poem in the book is "Twentieth Century," a prospective elegy, jaunty and nostalgic, for our "time of marvels": "Twentieth century, don't lie to us. / We love you and you are leaving forever."

*Fate* is the fourth book of poems by Ai, a poet as unusual as her name. She is an extremist of the spirit, a kind of hot-blooded answer to Andy Warhol. She writes about the same public-domain personalities that attracted Warhol, but with a shriek of passion where Warhol's technique was sublimely cool. Some of her poems would benefit from close editing. The last three lines of Ai's Lenny Bruce poem—"Boys and Girls, Lenny Bruce, or Back from the Dead"—are terrific (though unprintable in a family newspaper), but much of the rest of that poem's concluding section is dross. On the other hand, there is no one in contemporary poetry who sounds quite like her, and when she is good, she is spectacularly good.

*Fate* consists primarily of dramatic monologues. An author's note informs us that the book "is about eroticism, politics, religion, and show business as tragicomedy, performed by women and men banished to the bare stage of their obsessions." The players fated to rehearse their obsessions in striking soliloquys include, besides Lenny Bruce, such other American icons as George Armstrong Custer, Jimmy Hoffa, James Dean, and Elvis Presley. Lyndon Johnson tells us he "was king of comedy, /

before I abdicated." Mary Jo Kopechne returns from the dead for a serious chat with the "fat and jowly" senior senator from Massachusetts. "All right," she says, "I'll say it plainly. / Jack or Bobby would have died with me. / Think of publicity, the headlines— / you'd have been a hero."

The poem in *Fate* that absolutely knocked me out is "Evidence: From a Reporter's Notebook," about a case of alleged rape that strongly resembles the Tawana Brawley affair, which made front page headlines several years ago. (Brawley, a young black woman, claimed she was raped by white men amid mounting evidence that she had made up the whole horrible story.) Ai confirms, in a note on the poem in *The Best American Poetry 1991*, that it is "loosely based" on Brawley but adds that she lifted certain particulars of her plot from an obscure movie about a hard-nosed reporter who will do anything for a story. In Ai's poem, the TV reporter and the alleged rape victim use each other, and if there is something obscene about the transaction, that is partly because of the nature of their mutual obsession and partly because they are performing before our greedy prurient eyes, "each show a rehearsal for the afternoon / when with a cry / she spreads her chocolate thighs / while I kneel down to look, / but still I find no evidence / of racist's or even boyfriend's semen. / I press my fingers hard against her, / then hold them up before the audience, / wet only with the thick spit of my betrayal."

Ai (herself a black woman) sums up the case—and reveals one of the ground rules of her own poetry—when she remarks that "the lens through which we view the truth / is often cracked and filthy with the facts."

Tom Disch's motto might be "the sun also / surprises," as he puts it in one of the poems in his *Dark Verses and Light*. In his poetry as in his science-fiction—he has written several classics in that genre—Disch is noted for his wit and invention. He has a jubilant game-playing approach to poetic form, a flair for clever internal rhymes, and an ability to stretch a poetic conceit to its limits. *Dark Verses and Light* contains many happy reminders of Disch's versatility. There is "Orientating Mr. Blank," a sestina, in which an officious bureaucrat explains how to achieve true mediocrity in poetry. There are the rhymed stanzas of "Fool's Mate," which involves "you" in the plot of a computer novel somewhat like the one Disch himself has written. And every so often, there is the exclamatory climax—a tie that "is an entire Hawaiian shirt / condensed into one dazzling rhombus!"—that makes one aware of the affinity between Disch and Kenneth Koch, another underrated comic genius.

"The Joycelin Shrager Poems," my favorite piece in the book, is a parody of three things at once: the Beat movement, the downtown New York poetry scene in the sixties and seventies, and the popularity of poetry-writing workshops devoted to "taking a class of fourth or fifth graders and turning the lot of them into Little-League Robert Lowells." First Disch serves up, in prose, "The Joycelin Shrager Story," about the heroine's days as a talentless underground filmmaker. Then we get a mock introduction to her poetry by a jerky workshop leader. The poems follow and they are hilarious, being sublimely terrible. In the one titled "minor poets are human too"—remember when lowercase letters were a must?—Joycelin muses on Wallace Stevens's profession, which she thinks is "insurance salesman." She wonders how he had the energy for poetry after a hard day's "canvassing." Since her father briefly did the same thing for the same company, she has her epiphany for the day: "everything connects / mysteriously to everything else / in the world of the spirit." Even better is the poem beginning "my assignment this week is a sonnet" in which Joycelin explains that it's easy to write one: "it doesn't have to rime / as long as it has exactly 14 lines / it'll be ok." Warming up, she defines poetry—hers, anyway—as "a kind of newsletter / about yr inner secrets." The poem comes out to seventeen lines, but Joycelin isn't going to worry about that. After all, as she breathlessly observes, "the basic unit of / modern poetry is the human breath divine." It's a camp masterpiece.

With all that he has accomplished, in so many different fields of writing, it is a wonder that Disch has not yet attained the wide public recognition that is bound to catch up with him sooner or later.

# Mark Strand's Dark Land

Favored by fortune, Mark Strand won recognition early on as one of the foremost poets of his generation. Great things were routinely expected of him. His lyrical and rhetorical gifts went together with a painter's eye and a connoisseur's disposition, as was clear from his first two collections, *Sleeping with One Eye Open* (1964) and *Reasons for Moving* (1968). In addition to poems, he wrote prose books, art books, and books for children, edited anthologies, and translated from the Portuguese, and he did all these things well.

Strand had no trouble mastering two of the signature styles of the late sixties and early seventies: the surrealistic (dark or impish, and sometimes dark *and* impish) and the spartan (curt, austere, and strict). In time, these poetic strategies would deposit him at the end of a dead-end street, and in the eighties he entered a prolonged dry spell when he seemed to have lost his voice. I suspect that for Strand this crisis was rather like those described in romantic odes by Wordsworth and Coleridge—a crisis of faith to be triumphantly resolved in the end by an act of affirmative imagination.

Strand snapped out of a decade-long silence with the best poems of his life—the poems collected in *The Continuous Life* (1990), a spectacularly good volume, now in paperback. *Dark Harbor,* his new book-length poem, is continuous with its predecessor in theme and manner, and surpasses it as an act of sustained literary grace.

In "Keeping Things Whole," his most famous early poem,

---

Review of *Dark Harbor,* by Mark Strand. *Chicago Tribune,* August 1, 1993.

Strand wrote: "In a field / I am the absence / of field. / This is / always the case. / Wherever I am / I am what is missing." These lines were treated by critics and commentators as though they were the poet's *cri de coeur*. That was nearly thirty years ago. In Strand's recent work, the negative presence that felt itself to be a displacement of airy molecules has prepared the way for a rich profusion of imaginings.

In *Dark Harbor* Strand remains committed to the task of negotiating, in verse, between desire and despair, possibility and fulfillment. On occasion he still resorts almost reflexively to a negating gesture ("I am writing from a place you have never been, / Where the trains don't run, and planes / Don't land"). What is new in his new work is the confidence of his speech, the extraordinary clarity with which he addresses any poet's biggest themes: love and death and aging and change.

*Dark Harbor* consists of forty-five sections of varying lengths. Each section can be read as an independent poem. The book is written entirely in unrhymed three-line stanzas strongly suggestive of the unit favored by Strand's acknowledged master, Wallace Stevens, in several of his great later poems. Indeed, *Dark Harbor* may be Strand's response to *The Auroras of Autumn,* in which Stevens spoke his "farewell to an idea"—an idea pictured as a deserted cabin on a beach. Here is Strand on the same theme in *Dark Harbor*. This is section sixteen in its entirety:

> It is true, as someone has said, that in
> A world without heaven all is farewell.
> Whether you wave your hand or not,
>
> It is farewell, and if no tears come to your eyes
> It is still farewell, and if you pretend not to notice,
> Hating what passes, it is still farewell.
>
> Farewell no matter what. And the palms as they lean
> Over the green, bright lagoon, and the pelicans
> Diving, and the glistening bodies of bathers resting,
>
> Are stages in an ultimate stillness, and the movement
> Of sand, and of wind, and the secret moves of the body
> Are part of the same, a simplicity that turns being

Into an occasion for mourning, or into an occasion
Worth celebrating, for what else does one do,
Feeling the weight of the pelicans' wings,

The density of the palms' shadows, the cells that darken
The backs of bathers? These are beyond the distortions
Of chance, beyond the evasions of music. The end

Is enacted again and again. And we feel it
In the temptations of sleep, in the moon's ripening,
In the wine as it waits in the glass.

The artful repetition, the dramatic tempo, are characteristic of the poet—as is the verbal gusto, the way lament turns into celebration and an abstract argument is superseded by the imagery supposed to illustrate it. In the ebb and flow of his three-line stanzas, Strand has found the right measure for a meditative style capable of intensity and compression but also of a certain expansiveness.

"The greatest poverty is not to live in a physical world," Stevens wrote, and Strand's poetry is in some sense an elaboration of that sentiment. His work is unabashedly dedicated to the pursuit of the good life—and to the project of testing the extent to which it is possible to lead that life. One can well imagine him contemplating death or the abyss—while holding a half-full wine glass on a balcony overlooking a Mediterranean beach in winter. In *Dark Harbor* we see glimpses of the poet celebrating "how good life / Has been and how it has culminated in this instant," lunching with his editor at Lutèce, then striding along the pavement, well fed, lanky, in his "new dark blue double-breasted suit" or his "father's velvet smoking jacket." He is a poet of glamour (for whom light is "the mascara of Eden") and romance ("The feel of kisses blown out of heaven, / Melting the moment they land").

Some critics charge that Strand writes beautifully but has little to say. He arouses a certain amount of resentment in those who think he should feel guilty about his pleasures. As the nation's fourth official Poet Laureate, Strand took part in a number of panel discussions devoted to the problems of contemporary poetry. At one such, somebody quoted the famous question posed by the German philosopher Theodor Adorno: "How can one write poems after Auschwitz?" Strand retorted: "How can one eat lunch after Auschwitz?"

Strand's point is that poetry may be as necessary as lunch—and that one "cannot," yet one does, enjoy one's pleasures despite the knowledge of the horrors the human race has committed. This seems to me a sensible response to Adorno's grandiloquent question, which rests on too narrow a notion of poetry's aims and obligations. Are poems about Orpheus or angels—Strand writes about both, as did Rilke—necessarily evasions of Auschwitz? And if they are, why should that damn them? Poetry does have a moral dimension, but it is not a moral instrument exclusively. Nor is what Auschwitz represents the whole of our morality.

Strand's poetry is a vehicle of the moral imagination simply because it amply accommodates the world of material things as well as the animating impulses of the spirit. Like one of the resuscitated poets described on the last page of *Dark Harbor,* Strand is now "ready to say the words [he] had been unable to say— / Words whose absence had been the silence of love." Mortality as a fact and as the name of our chief fear is the base condition of his new work. Continuous is the need to say farewell to the things that require, and requite, a poet's attention. Death is the mother of beauty; poetry is a valediction forbidding mourning.

The book's penultimate poem, my own favorite, is a remarkable example of a "moralized landscape," in which the sea and the mountains embody different aspects of the human condition. The noise of the breaking waves had once frightened him, writes Strand,

> But in those days what did I know of the pleasures of loss,
> Of the edge of the abyss coming close with its hisses
> And storms, a great watery animal breaking itself on the
>    rocks,
>
> Sending up stars of salt, loud clouds of spume.

# Who Killed Edwin Drood?

Few riddles can compete with a great novelist's unfinished murder mystery. Charles Dickens had written half of *The Mystery of Edwin Drood* when death interrupted him at the age of fifty-eight in June 1870. He left us an artistic fragment not quite as haunting as Kafka's *Amerika* or Shelley's "The Triumph of Life" but infinitely more conducive to debate. The unfinished manuscript has the makings of an admirable novel, and perhaps a great one, quite apart from its unsolved mysteries, which have caused quantities of ink to be spilled. Add that *The Mystery of Edwin Drood* grants us a stop-action look at the creative mind in motion—how the dickens would he have ended it?—and it becomes irresistible.

A whole literature has grown up around *Drood,* including periodic attempts to produce a plausible conclusion for the book, whether in a pastiche of Dickens's style or in some contemporary idiom. In 1985, a Broadway musical based on *Drood* opted for a postmodernist solution: at each performance, the audience determined the outcome. This year's entry in the Drood sweepstakes is equally postmodernist. *The D. Case: The Truth about the Mystery of Edwin Drood,* written collaboratively by Carlo Fruttero and Franco Lucentini, a pair of veteran Italian authors who have teamed up before on mystery novels, springs from a literary conceit. In *The D. Case,*

---

Review of *The D. Case: The Truth about the Mystery of Edwin Drood,* by Charles Dickens, Carlo Fruttero, and Franco Lucentini. The Italian chapters translated by Gregory Dowling. Published in the *New York Times Book Review,* July 5, 1992, under the title "Round Up the Usual Suspects."

the world's greatest fictional detectives—Sherlock Holmes, Hercule Poirot, Father Brown, Inspector Maigret, Philip Marlowe, Nero Wolfe, Lew Archer, and others—convene in Rome to solve Dickens's posthumous puzzles at a conference sponsored by the Japanese. Mr. Fruttero and Mr. Lucentini print the surviving chapters of *The Mystery of Edwin Drood* interspersed with their own gently satirical reports from Rome, where the famous sleuths disport themselves like professors at a Modern Language Association convention, trying to elucidate the enigmas of Dickens's text without fatally obscuring its pleasure.

Dickens's manuscript breaks off shortly after the disappearance of the title character. Drood, a nice young man, and Rosa Bud, the last in the line of "amiable, giddy, wilful, winning little creatures" in Dickens, have been pledged to one another by their deceased parents. The two are not in love and decide to call off their engagement, but before they can announce the news, Drood vanishes. Has he been killed, and if so, by whom? Or has he gone into hiding to escape his sinister uncle, John Jasper, an opium-smoking choirmaster and his secret rival for Rosa, and if so, whose corpse is about to turn up in the heavily foreshadowed quicklime? Who is Datchery, the obviously disguised stranger who comes to town to spy on Jasper? Who is the Princess Puffer, in whose opium den the narrative begins, and why does she hate Jasper so fiercely?

The little evidence we have of Dickens's intentions suggests that the book would have ended with Jasper's confession in a prison cell, perhaps in an opium reverie, perhaps under hypnosis, but this likelihood has scarcely deterred armchair sleuths from coming up with ingenious alternatives.

The detectives in *The D. Case* are really literary critics in disguise. They seem to favor an intertextualist approach to *The Mystery of Edwin Drood,* and it is shrewd of them to observe that Dickens set out to top his former friend and current rival, Wilkie Collins, who two years earlier had published *The Moonstone*—the first detective novel in English. Like Collins's book, *Drood* has a strong whiff of opium, plenty of supernatural hocus-pocus, a trace of esoteric orientalism, and the premise that, in Dickens's words, a person may have "two states of consciousness which never clash, but each of which pursues its separate course as though it were continuous instead of broken." Set in Cloisterham, an English cathedral town like the Rochester of Dickens's own boyhood, *Drood* is nothing if not a richly imagined excursion into the realm of the uncanny.

Mr. Fruttero and Mr. Lucentini use their detectives as mouthpieces for various hypotheses. Edmund Wilson in *The Wound and the Bow* (1941) advanced the theory that Jasper, the novel's dominating presence, is properly to be understood as a prototype for such Jekyll-and-Hyde, split-personality protagonists as Raskolnikov in *Crime and Punishment*. Accordingly, it is Porfiry Petrovich, the detective who foils Raskolnikov in Dostoyevski's novel, that gets to make this point in *The D. Case*.

Most theories about the Drood case assume Jasper's guilt. In 1964 the English actor Felix Aylmer made the revolutionary suggestion that Drood, alive and in hiding, mistakenly supposes that his uncle attacked him when what has really happened is that Drood was attacked by a hired assassin who was then killed by Jasper. Mr. Fruttero and Mr. Lucentini go further with the impulse to clear Jasper's name. They entertain the notion that the Landless twins, Helena and Neville—who, Dickens tells us, communicate by telepathy—are Drood's murderers. According to this view, Helena, Rosa's bosom friend, becomes Lady Macbeth egging on her vacillating brother. But Neville is so obviously the fall guy—with the means (a heavy walking stick), the motive (jealousy over Rosa), and the opportunity (a postprandial stroll in the dark with the victim), plus a hot temper and no alibi—that readers wise to the ways of the genre will find it hard to believe that Dickens cast him as the killer.

*The D. Case* is an easy way to bone up on Droodiana, even if the authors don't capitalize fully on the cleverness of their critic-as-detective conceit. The sleuths are there basically for decor, and some are reduced to crude stereotype; Philip Marlowe and Lew Archer are interchangeable as oafish boors who sneer a lot, head for the hooch at every opportunity, and don't get off a memorable wisecrack between them.

Mr. Fruttero and Mr. Lucentini clearly cast their lot with the school of Agatha and artifice. Poirot trumps everybody when he asserts, as *The D. Case* comes to a close, that Dickens's death was the result of foul play. Was Dickens murdered by the one person who wanted at all costs to prevent him from finishing *Drood*?

The status of *Edwin Drood* as a crime classic is resented by some of Dickens's fervent fans, who argue that the book is misread if considered as a whodunit rather than as a psychological drama. It is certainly the case that here, as elsewhere in Dickens, the vagaries of the plot are secondary in interest to the mysteries of character and circumstance. On the other hand, what is the harm in regarding this unfinished novel in the context of detective fiction or as an exhibit in a graduate seminar? The British novelist Angus Wilson once called for a moratorium on new endings for Dickens's last book. But he underestimated the considerable extent to which academic literary criticism resembles a parlor game. As *The D. Case* confirms, *The Mystery of Edwin Drood* was made to order for contemporary adventurers in textual interpretation.

# The Ern Malley Poetry Hoax

The greatest literary hoax of the twentieth century was perpetrated by a couple of Australian soldiers at their desks in the offices of the Victoria Barracks, land headquarters of the Australian army, on a quiet Saturday in October 1943. The uniformed noncombatants, Lieutenant James MacAuley and Corporal Harold Stewart, were a pair of Sydney poets with a shared animus toward modern poetry in general and a particular hatred of the surrealist stuff championed by Adelaide wunderkind Max Harris, the twenty-two-year-old editor of *Angry Penguins,* a well-heeled journal devoted to the spread of modernism down under.

In a single rollicking afternoon McAuley and Stewart cooked up the collected works of Ernest Lalor Malley. Imitating the modern poets they most despised ("not Max Harris in particular, but the whole literary fashion as we knew it from the works of Dylan Thomas, Henry Treece, and others"), they rapidly wrote the sixteen poems that constitute Ern Malley's "tragic lifework." They lifted lines at random from the books and papers on their desks (Shakespeare, a dictionary of quotations, an American report on the breeding grounds of mosquitoes, and so on). They mixed in false allusions and misquotations, dropped "confused and inconsistent hints at a meaning" in place of a coherent theme, and deliberately produced what they thought was bad verse. They called their creation Malley

---

Review of *The Ern Malley Affair,* by Michael Heyward, published in the *Washington Post Book World,* March 6, 1994. I have added several paragraphs from a piece I wrote on Ern Malley for *The Poetry Pilot* of the Academy of American Poets, January–February 1992.

because *mal* in French means bad. He was Ernest because they were not.

Later, the hoaxers added a high-sounding "preface and statement," outfitted Malley with a tear-jerking biography, and created his suburban sister, Ethel. The invention of Ethel was a masterstroke. It was she who sent Malley's posthumous opus, *The Darkening Ecliptic*, to Max Harris along with a cover letter tinged with her disapproval of her brother's bohemian ways and proclaiming her own ignorance of poetry. Ern (she wrote) had been born in England in 1918, was taken to Australia after his father's death two years later, and was left in Ethel's care after their mother died when he was fifteen. Having dropped out of school, the young man worked as a garage mechanic in Sydney and later as an insurance salesman and part-time watch repairman in Melbourne. In 1943 he returned to Sydney, where he died of "Grave's Disease."

Artless Ethel, the bourgeois philistine, had the effect of authenticating Ern's poignant existence. The simplicity of her account inspired Harris to construct the narrative of a poet, who burned Keats-like in a flame snuffed out before its time. "The weeks before he died were terrible," Ethel wrote. "Sometimes he would be all right and he would talk to me. From things he said I gathered he had been fond of a girl in Melbourne, but had some sort of difference with her. I didn't want to ask him too much because he was nervy and irritable. The crisis came suddenly, and he passed away on Friday the 23rd of July. As he wished, he was cremated at Rookwood."

Ern Malley was just what the avant-garde ordered: a tragic hero. His poems were charged with the premonition of an early death and the conviction that poetic greatness would be his if he could live five more winters. MacAuley and Stewart saw to it that Malley, like Keats, had died at the age of twenty-five. "Now in your honour Keats, I spin / the loaded Zodiac with my left hand / As the man at the fair revolves / His coloured deceitful board," Malley writes in "Colloquy with John Keats." And,

> Like you I sought at first for Beauty
> And then, in disgust, returned

As did you to the locus of sensation
And not till then did my voice build crenellated towers
Of an enteric substance in the air.

Amid the red herrings scattered in the poems, McAuley and Stewart did sprinkle a few genuine clues to the mystery of Ern Malley. From "Sybilline," for example, these splendid lines hint at Malley's ghostly nature:

It is necessary to understand
That a poet may not exist, that his writings
Are the incomplete circle and straight drop
Of a question mark
And yet I know I shall be raised up
On the vertical banners of praise.

It was, however, possible to take these lines metaphorically as the dying man's vision of impending oblivion and posthumous applause.

Malley is a comedian of the spirit, who wards off self-pity with defiant irony. But he also has a prophetic voice and a grave historical vision, as in these haunting lines from "Petit Testament": "But where I have lived / Spain weeps in the gutters of Footscray / Guernica is the ticking of a clock / The nightmare has become real, not as belief / But in the scrub-typhus of Mubo." And he is capable of the pure lyric outcry. Here is the second stanza of "Sweet William":

One moment of daylight let me have
Like a white arm thrust
Out of a dark and self-denying wave
And in the one moment I
Shall irremediably attest
How (though with sobs, and torn cries bleeding)
My white swan of quietness lies
Sanctified on my black swan's breast.

Harris fell for Malley hook, line, and sinker. So did his patrons and chums, including the painter Sidney Nolan, who would become the most celebrated Australian painter of his generation. They devoted the next issue of *Angry Penguins* to their excited discovery—and were promptly ambushed by the hoax's exposure in the press in June 1944. Although this was scarcely a slow news summer—the Normandy invasion took place in June, the liberation of Paris in August—the story spread rapidly to England and America, and everywhere the reaction was the same: high hilarity at the expense of the *Angry Penguins,* the humiliation of Max Harris, a colossal setback for modernism in Australia. The hoax was, as Michael Heyward points out in *The Ern Malley Affair,* a decisive act of literary criticism, brilliant parody in the service of fierce polemic. If, as MacAuley and Stewart insisted, the poems had no merit, then Malley's champions had convicted themselves of unsound judgment and corrupt taste.

But the story doesn't end there. Stranger turns were to follow. The South Australian police impounded the issue of *Angry Penguins* devoted to "The Darkening Ecliptic" on the grounds that Malley's poems were obscene, though in fact their erotic content was negligible when compared with, say, *Tropic of Cancer* or *Ulysses.* The court case that September featured some inadvertently hilarious testimony from a dunderhead police detective who didn't know the meaning of the words he thought were indecent.

The wondrous twist in the Ern Malley story was the surprising, and actually quite heroic, intransigence of Max Harris and his cohorts, who maintained in the face of all ridicule their belief in Malley's genius. "The myth is sometimes greater than its creator," said Harris. Sir Herbert Read, tireless in his advocacy of vanguard art, wired his support from England. It seemed to him that the hoaxers had been "hoisted on their own petard." It was, Read reasoned, possible to arrive at genuine art by spurious means—even if the motive of the writer was to perpetuate a travesty. In time others have come to share this view, and it is clear that the tide in Australia has turned in their favor. The editors of the new *Penguin Book of Modern Australian Poetry* (1992) elected to include *all* of Malley's poems in their anthology.

Ern Malley has always had an honored place among the poets of the New York School. Kenneth Koch printed two

Malley poems, "Boult to Marina" and "Sybilline," in the "collaborations" issue of *Locus Solus*, the avant-garde literary magazine, in 1961. At Columbia University in 1968, Koch introduced his writing students to Malley's poetry, suggesting that the hoaxer's antics were well worth imitating not for purposes of polemic but for legitimate poetic ends. In 1976 John Ashbery asked his MFA students at Brooklyn College to compare Malley's "Sweet William" to one of Geoffrey Hill's *Mercian Hymns*. Which did they think was the genuine article? (The students were divided.) Ashbery's point—and it seems to be Malley's point—is that intentions may be irrelevant to results, that genuineness in literature may not depend on authorial sincerity, and that our ideas about *good* and *bad, real* and *fake*, are, or ought to be, in flux.

One half of Ern Malley is still alive. I visited Harold Stewart in Kyoto in 1990. A genteel septuagenarian in a shabby gray suit, he has lived in Kyoto for a quarter of a century. He is a Buddhist and an autodidact, immensely learned about his adopted city, and he has published several books of poetry, including a book of haiku. "I was born in the year of the fire dragon and I eat a modernist poet for breakfast every morning," he warned me with a mock-growl as he showed me the Sanjusangendo temple in Kyoto. He became "Uncle Harold" very quickly despite suspecting that I was, in fact, a spy from the ultra-modernist faction out there. "Considering the ease with which you produced Ern Malley, didn't you ever have the impulse to write more poems in that vein?" I asked. "No," he thundered. It was a joke, a lark, a way of getting at "an arrogant group of modernists."

Much as I like and admire Stewart, I think he is wrong in that judgment. The Ern Malley affair was the century's greatest literary hoax not because it completely hoodwinked Harris and not because it triggered off a story so rich in ironies and reversals. It was the greatest hoax because Ern Malley escaped the control of his creators and enjoyed an autonomous existence beyond, and at odds with, the critical and satirical intentions of MacAuley and Stewart. They succeeded better than they knew or wished to know. Malley's poems hold up to this day, eclipsing anything produced by any of the story's main protagonists *in propria persona.*

Crazy as it seems, the Malley poems do have merit. In a poem written during World War II the French poet Robert Desnos pictures himself as "the shadow among shadows" poised to "enter and reenter your sunny life." This is Malley's self-conception, too. His gallows humor, self-lacerating irony, and odd arresting juxtapositions contribute to an effect that other poets of the period strove for but few attained so unerringly as this speaker of "No-Man's-language appropriate / Only to No-Man's-Land." "Petit Testament," Malley's last poem, concludes with these lines: "I / Who have lived in the shadow that each act / Casts on the next act now emerge / As loyal as the thistle that in session / Puffs its full seed upon the indicative air. / I have split the infinitive. Beyond is anything." A misprint in the first edition changed *infinitive* to *infinite* in the last line. I would be very curious to know which version of the line admirers of Ern Malley—and readers of this essay— prefer.[1]

## NOTE

1. A number of readers wrote letters registering their preference after this piece appeared in the *Washington Post.* One man, voting for *infinite,* called it the "serendipitous" choice, the one created by hazard at some variance from the hoaxers' intentions. Moreover, he wrote, to "split the infinite" is a "fresh idea" that "boggles the mind." Another correspondent, a publisher, felt that *infinitive* was "infinitely preferable" to *infinite,* "which it contains by implication (the verb split being 'to be')." Readers also pointed out that "infinitive" rhymes with "indicative" in the previous line and refers to the same grammatical paradigm. The mail ran fifty-fifty.

# Cynthia Ozick's Messiah

Cynthia Ozick's new novella is loaded with ironies, big and little. Lars Andemening, the forty-two-year-old protagonist of *The Messiah of Stockholm*, writes a book column for a Swedish newspaper, the *Morgontorn*. When writing up Lars's story, Ozick couldn't have known that she'd soon be similarly employed: last January she became a regular monthly contributor to *The New York Times Book Review*. In her first "About Books" column Ozick expressed her unease with the kind of "postmodernist inconstancy" on display in such novels as Philip Roth's *The Counterlife*, whose characters "keep revising their speeches and their fates." Yet *The Messiah of Stockholm*, like much of Ozick's fiction, plays fast and loose with narrative rules and seems positively postmodernist in its determination to keep the reader off-balance. And to whom is *The Messiah of Stockholm* dedicated? Philip Roth.

This gets us to the largest irony, the profoundest paradox, in Ozick's enterprise—in the literary journalism collected in *Art and Ardor* (1983) as in her fiction. If there's one thing she insists upon, it's that idolatry is evil and idols need to be smashed. Again and again she returns to the second of the Ten Commandments, the one prohibiting the worship of false gods and graven images. Ozick widens the prohibition until it encompasses art itself—or, at any rate, art for art's sake. As she sees it, the "Attic jug" that announced to Keats that "Beauty is Truth, Truth Beauty," is itself an idol, speaking falsehood. Nor are novelists to be trusted. Novelists are deceiv-

Review of *The Messiah of Stockholm*, by Cynthia Ozick, published in the *Partisan Review* (Summer 1987).

ers, not good citizens, she writes in a recent *Times* column. At times she sounds perilously close to the civic-minded philosopher who banished the poets from his ideal republic on the grounds that poets specialize in irrational enchantment. So where exactly does this put Ozick's own fiction, particularly a work like *The Messiah of Stockholm,* whose texture is that of a fable and whose plot appeals to our appetite for irrational enchantment?

In short, Ozick the moralist has put Ozick the artist in the self-contradictory position of a knights-or-knaves game of logic: she is the truthteller who says, "Don't believe me, I'm a liar." A skeptic might say that Ozick's fiction follows a recipe for eating your cake and having it, too. Putting your art at the service of an admonition against art leaves you in a cruel metaphysical dilemma: by what dispensation are your works spared from the indictment? The paradox is complete when we observe that the only legitimate defense of Ozick's position is one that her own critical principles would require her to reject. It could be argued that Ozick's fiction needn't conform to her critical propositions; that if it exposes the limitations of those propositions, so much the better; that it isn't the responsibility of the fiction writer to resolve the logical conundrums that preoccupy her, intractable as they are. It is enough to explore them in fiction of such flesh-and-blood immediacy that the writer's more-or-less private obsession turns into a metaphor in which we are all in some ways implicated. In sum, *The Messiah of Stockholm* doesn't solve the problem that energizes it, but permissive readers aren't likely to complain. Moral ambiguities are more to our liking than moral absolutes, after all—especially when the author fulfills, as Ozick does, the writer's real categorical imperative: to enchant us, whether with truths or half-truths or supreme fictions.

*The Messiah of Stockholm* lends itself well enough to paraphrase, though a casualty of the exercise is the surface delight of Ozick's prose. We find ourselves in the literary "stewpot" of Stockholm—a setting that has the advantage of seeming at once remote from our Manhattan cauldron yet upon inspection curiously like it. That the Nobel Prize in Literature is conferred in Stockholm gives us a hint of the stakes involved in the parable Ozick spins out. Lars Andemening, an obscure and rather seedy specimen of the literary life, may seem an anachronistic vestige of an age of idealism; his bohemianism takes the form of an ascetic ideal. Lars uncompromisingly devotes his weekly book column to Eastern European writers rather than to books of topical interest. He is content with his lack of public consequence, for he is convinced his destiny is worth waiting for. It's his belief—or is it fantasy?—that his father was Bruno Schulz, the martyred author of *The Street of Crocodiles* and *Sanitarium under the Sign of the Hourglass.*

So credibly does Ozick create an atmosphere of deception that the individual who previewed *The Messiah of Stockholm* for *Publishers Weekly* decided that Schulz must be her invention. Let it be said at once, therefore, that Schulz did in fact live and die; a Polish Jew, he was murdered by a member of the SS in the street in his Galician village in 1942. Schulz had worked on a long-thought-lost last manuscript, a novel titled *The Messiah;* that, too, is fact. Lars is sure *The Messiah* will turn up, sure he is meant to bring it forth. He gathers an ally in the proprietress of a rare book shop, devotes hours to the study of Polish, and waits. It's a Jamesian situation, a conjunction of "The Beast in the Jungle" and *The Aspern Papers,* and Ozick follows it ultimately to a Jamesian conclusion. In the end, illusions are smashed, but not without a fight and not without an acute pang of anguish and more than a few lingering doubts.

But having established a setting plausible enough to serve a satirical novel of manners, Ozick gives the plot a magical turn of the screw. A manuscript appears, brought by a young woman who claims to be Schulz's daughter, Adela. The tale of the manuscript's survival has the strangeness of folklore about it. And Schulz's *Messiah* itself is the more wondrous for appearing to be an extrapolation from Schulz's own published writing that yet closely resembles the quintessential Ozick dreamscape: a deserted village full of idol shops, rather like the one in which the patriarch Abraham's father toiled. According to one commentary upon *Genesis,* Abraham smashed the idols one day in his father's absence, then claimed the idols did it themselves; his father is incredulous at this explanation, and that clinches Abraham's case. If they are incapable of doing such a thing, why worship them? The idols in Schulz's alleged *Messiah*, however, are unattended by Abraham or, indeed, by any other human agent. Taking matters into their own hands, lacking human sacrifices, they demolish each other until the Messiah descends, releasing a bird with a bit of straw in its beak. One touch of the straw and each of the idols in turn dissolves.

To divulge too many more particulars of Ozick's plot would be unpardonable. Suffice it to say that a hoax manuscript turns into something quite different, and rather more chastening, when it is burned; that the loss of an illusion can mean, as it does for Lars, that the promise of brilliance will mature into mediocrity; and that the book's last words—"he grieved"—reverberate in the reader's mind with the same power as, say, the word "expired" has at the end of Bernard Malamud's "The Silver Crown," a story Ozick is known to admire. (She refashioned its elements quite cunningly in "Usurpation," probably the best story in her 1976 collection *Bloodshed*.)

Even so brief a plot summary will suggest how central a tale *The Messiah of Stockholm* is for Ozick. As a psychological drama, it works by Jamesian indirection and nuance to raise a troubling question: when is Lars better off, when he is deluded and obsessed or when, having overcome his delusions, he overcomes, too, his high calling, stops writing about obscure Eastern European writers, and starts to enjoy a journalist's popular success? But if the novella confirms Ozick's sense of herself as a disciple of Henry James, it is also a rather complicated act of fealty to Bruno Schulz: it usurps Schulz's writings by way of extending their posthumous life. Moreover, it offers us an astonishingly apt metaphor for the false messiah: a book that can tell the truth despite the spurious nature of its provenance. It chastises us for the ease with which we can succumb to chicanery, and at the same time it reminds us of our spiritual poverty, which makes us yearn to find fit objects for our veneration. And we are right to pause over the book's dedication to Philip Roth. It was meant, Ozick told me, to signify her gratitude to Roth, the general editor of Penguin's "Writers from the Other Europe" series, to whose sponsorship of

Bruno Schulz we owe our awareness of that estimable author. But for all her qualms about postmodernism, Ozick (who confesses she "admired like mad" Roth's *The Counterlife*) has an affinity with Roth that goes beyond their shared interest in Eastern European writers. Call it a Judaic imperative: an obsessive need to explore the place where the moral and aesthetic impulses act upon each other, sometimes in concert, more often in opposition.

What is most impressive about *The Counterlife*, what lifts it above even *The Ghost Writer* as a literary achievement, is that it harnesses the full array of postmodernist devices—the false-bottomed narrative, the multiplication of counterfeit actualities and alternative possibilities, "what-could-be having always to top what-is"—not as ingenious ends in themselves and not merely to serve an inquiry into the puzzling relations between fiction and reality. No, Roth interrupts his narrative and brings his characters back from the dead, letting them revise their speeches and their fates, for a purpose that must be characterized as moral. The middle-aged dentist dies during heart surgery, or the same dentist recovers, abandons his New Jersey practice and family, and emigrates to Israel, where he joins the Gush Emunim settlement of a charismatic zealot—either scenario is valid not only as a metaphysical possibility but as a moral predicament. The dentist's initial dilemma, for instance, brilliantly dramatizes the moral implications of Freud's argument in *Beyond the Pleasure Principle*. In the man's decision to undergo a life-endangering heart operation rather than continue to live without his sexual potency, we see—to put it in its most reductive terms—the fatal alliance of Eros and Thanatos, and we see it as inevitable, irresistible, the self's anarchic refusal to subordinate its instinctual desires to the mandates of civilization.

Ozick, too, stands her characters in the path between opposing mirrors in *The Messiah of Stockholm*. Here, again, the reliability of the narrative is in constant doubt. Each of the major characters is, it gradually unfolds, an impostor, though we're never meant to be entirely clear as to where the real identity of Lars Andemening ends and his fantasy self takes over. There is something pitiable as well as grotesque about such a character—and the superb aesthetic effects that Ozick achieves with her false *Messiah* do not cheapen his predicament but charge it with intensity. The fixation on Bruno Schulz, the willingness to be hoaxed, then the astonished and astonishing rejection of the hoax, the withdrawal from the dream at the very moment when it appears to be coming true: what else is this but a parable of the imaginative life, its lure, its limits, and its costs? Like Roth, Ozick strives to explore, in all its complexity, the interplay between writing as a species of artistic invention and writing as a way of keeping a sacred covenant. These rival conceptions of the writer's vocation co-exist at best in an uneasy detente. But constant conflict can yield to periodic acts of reconciliation, as when, in a single publishing season, books of the imaginative strength of *The Counterlife* and *The Messiah of Stockholm* arrive.

# Philip Roth's Double

At the top of his game, Philip Roth is our Kafka: a Jewish comic genius able to spin a metaphysical joke to a far point of ingenuity—the point at which artistic paradox becomes moral or religious parable. In *The Ghost Writer, The Counterlife,* and now again in *Operation Shylock,* Roth has written novels of stunning originality and wild inventiveness—novels as brilliant as any American has produced in the latter part of our century.

Like John Updike, who may be the closest of his American contemporaries in both ambition and achievement, Roth is determined to present sex and religion as the twin sides of the human predicament. Obsessive, relentless, he has treated his great themes—sexual desire, American Judaism, the stern demands of the fathers, and the relation of fiction to truth on the one side and to the exigencies of social community on the other—with a satirist's pungency and a flair for high hilarity unmatched in our time. All this is on display in *Operation Shylock,* Roth's funniest book since he "put the id back in yid" in *Portnoy's Complaint.*

A master illusionist, Roth is adept at fooling the public into thinking that the outlandish fantasies in his fiction must reflect autobiographical fact. This ability has sometimes landed him in the soup. One still recalls the novelist's wince when a fellow guest on a late-night talk show, circa 1970, demurely refused to shake his hand, since she had in mind the putative uses to which that hand had been put in the "Whacking Off" portion of *Portnoy's Complaint.* That book was widely taken to

---

*Washington Post Book World,* March 14, 1993.

express the gripes of Roth, as if the name Portnoy were merely a paper-thin disguise.

In his quartet of books about Nathan Zuckerman, Roth went on to exploit—and finally explode—the assumption that fiction is verifiably autobiographical and must play by the rules of narrative law and order. *The Ghost Writer* (1979) cons readers into thinking that Anne Frank has survived the Holocaust and is living in America under an assumed name as the spiritual daughter of a novelist resembling Bernard Malamud. The result is a parable charged with irony about "the madness of art." More treacherous, *The Counterlife* (1987) lures readers down narrative trapdoors concealing greased chutes; here Roth gives his characters multiple fates, killing them off in one chapter, bringing them back to life in the next, in a hymn to fictive possibility.

*Operation Shylock* goes one step further in its postmodernist cunning. The chief conceit of this book blends the idea of the double (from ego psychology and gothic literature) with the idea of codependency (from contemporary psychobabble). It is 1988. The first stones of the Intifada have been thrown. A man who looks like Philip Roth and calls himself Philip Roth has turned up in Jerusalem and is busy making well-publicized, shock-the-censor pronouncements. The impersonator loudly advocates Diasporism, a sort of reverse Zionism, calling for the return of the Jews to the European nations that had, over the centuries, banished them.

The real Philip Roth, living with his real wife, the actress Claire Bloom, is in New York recovering from a breakdown caused by Halcion, a widely prescribed sedative known for wacky side effects, when he learns about the impostor. Aghast but also curious in the way of a novelist who has pondered the mysteries of human identity, he decides to fly to Israel to find out what's what. Call it, if you will, his Jewry duty.

Readers used to Roth's tricks will recognize what an unbeatable premise this is for his imagination. Is he the victim of a hoax, and is money the motive? Or is it just that he has stepped into the realm of Ariel and art, where anything goes? Has he stumbled into an espionage conspiracy, a game of wits between agents of the Mossad and the PLO? Or is it possible that some portion of what happens to him in Israel is a drug-induced fantasy, evidence of a divided self?

All hell breaks loose when the real Philip Roth, seized by the imp of the perverse, pretends to be the impostor, and passionately espouses the exodus of the Jews back to Europe. A decrepit old man named Smilesburger—who turns out to be an Israeli version of spymaster George Smiley—slips him a one-million dollar check as a donation. Meanwhile, an irate Palestinian activist named George Ziad—a dormitory chum from the author's University of Chicago days, who left a Harvard professorship to take up Middle Eastern politics—wants to recruit the celebrated prophet of Diasporism for his cause. Might Ziad (a near-anagram for "Said") arrange a clandestine meeting in Athens between our feckless hero and the head of the PLO? "I assure you that Arafat can differentiate between Woody Allen and Philip Roth," Ziad says. "This was," Roth muses, "surely the strangest sentence I had ever heard spoken in my life."

There is equal room for parody and paranoia as the novelist gets to push around two characters named Philip Roth. In this maze of ambiguous identities, the "real" Roth attends the trial of John Demjanjuk, who maintains he is not Ivan the Terrible, perpetrator of atrocities at Treblinka. The fake Roth—existentially the novelist's anti-self—turns out prosaically to be a terminally ill Jewish private detective from Chicago specializing in missing persons. He has a buxomy blond Polish-American girlfriend, one Jinx Possesski, a type familiar to us from Portnoy's shiksa-chasing days. Jinx was born a Catholic, became a born-again Protestant, and is now a charter member of Anti-Semites Anonymous. The account of this organization in *Operation Shylock* is an inspired spoof of twelve-step programs, but it—like so much else in this novel—goes beyond parody to touch on the whole question of religious prejudice and the psychopathology of hate.

The final twist in a book full of them occurs with its final line. All along Roth has insisted that these events really did happen. He even warns us to disregard any author's note declaring that resemblance to actual persons is coincidental. When the author's note duly appears, it concludes with a sentence that logicians call the liar's paradox: "This confession is false." This perfect conundrum—which can be neither true nor false—refers not only to the disclaimer but to the book as a whole, which is, after all, subtitled "A Confession." It's a great ending.

*Operation Shylock* seems meant to disprove the author's famous pronouncement, made early in his career, that the self-satirizing genius of modern life outstrips the powers of any novelist to satirize it. Rather the reverse is the case: "no intelligence agency, however reckless, can rival a novelist's fantastical creations." This book is packed with memorable monologues, rants, and riffs on subjects ranging from Irving Berlin ("Easter he turns into a fashion show and Christmas into a holiday about snow") to the Jewish law prohibiting malicious speech. The bitter wisecracks add to the book's moral complexity. "There's no business like *Shoah* business," says Ziad, accusing Israel of cynically using the Holocaust to blackmail world opinion. An amazing anti-Semitic rant ("You know what a Jew is. A Jew's an Arab who was born in Poland") condemns what it funnily exemplifies. And when Leon Klinghoffer's travel diaries (forgeries, of course) turn up, Roth has the chance to mount a sort of rebuttal of John Adams's 1991 opera *The Death of Klinghoffer,* in which the terrorists on the *Achille Lauro* were depicted as heroic men of action while the Jews on the cruise came off as vulgar materialists.

*Operation Shylock* is a brave book, not only because it is sure to rile lots of people on both sides of the Israeli-Arab divide, but because "this narrative Ping-Pong in which I appear as the little white ball" extends the profound meditation on fiction and reality that the simple-minded among Roth's reviewers tend to dislike in his books. Phooey on them. I doubt that there will be a better novel published in 1993.

# Part 3

# Lives and Letters

# Janet Malcolm and the Problem of Biography

Janet Malcolm is among the most intellectually provocative of authors. A genuine iconoclast, she strews bold judgments in the reader's path with confidence bordering on impudence. Able to turn epiphanies of perception into explosions of insight, she may damn all journalists in a single universal clause or, to equal rhetorical effect, define a person's character on the basis of her reaction to a failed recipe. Controversy trails her like the clouds of glory following the blessed babe in Wordsworth's Immortality Ode.

In her last two books the whole thrust of Malcolm's effort has been directed at the writing profession—which, given her scrutiny, would seem to be very nearly as impossible a line of work as psychoanalysis, the subject of a pair of previous works by Malcolm. *The Silent Woman,* her new book, created a major buzz when it dominated a late-August issue of *The New Yorker* last year. In a strict sense, it is a literary essay on the rival merits of half a dozen biographies of the poet Sylvia Plath, all of them problematic, none of them satisfactory.

But *The Silent Woman* is much more than that. It is a double narrative in two time zones. One narrative centers on Plath's bleak last days and the unbearable emotional pressure that made possible her great outpouring of poetry but also led to her suicide at the age of thirty in February 1963. The second narrative concerns the fighting that ensued (and shows no signs of letting up) over the meaning of Plath's life and death.

*Boston Globe,* March 27, 1994.

The implacable animosity between Plath's hagiographers and Plath's husband, the often vilified Ted Hughes, who was conducting an adulterous affair at the time of her suicide, leads Malcolm to propose an "allegory of the problem of biography in general"—an allegory as trenchant and incisive as her earlier allegory of the problem of journalism, *The Journalist and the Murderer* (1990).

The first sentence of *The Journalist and the Murderer* has become justly famous: "Every journalist who is not too stupid or too full of himself to notice what is going on knows that what he does is morally indefensible." At a time when journalists have graduated to the status of media figures and are glamorized as never before, Malcolm depicts the very species as contemptible. The journalist is a "confidence man" who preys on "credulous widows," she writes in *The Journalist and the Murderer*. And as a parable designed to illustrate this truth, she tells the riveting story of a lawsuit brought by a convicted murderer (Jeffrey MacDonald) against the author of a bestselling book about the murder and the murder trial (Joe McGinniss). MacDonald claimed he had been conned by McGinniss into cooperating with him on *Fatal Vision,* only to be betrayed by him in the book.

For Malcolm, MacDonald's legal narrative was more compelling than the traditional defenses summoned in McGinniss's behalf. She had no trouble making the convicted killer's position seem more sympathetic and more reasonable than that of the swashbuckling, intrepid reporter. For her, moreover, this quite exceptional case represented the standard or norm for relations in general between people who write for a living and the people they write about. Her strong views on journalism did not endear her to some in the journalistic community, and they displayed their glee when Malcolm's theory seemed to be borne out inadvertently in the legal melodramas of her own life. When rogue psychoanalyst Jeffrey Masson took Malcolm to court for allegedly having misquoted him in a series of devastating articles exploring his ouster as curator of the Freud archives, he was charging her with the same bad faith that she found so odious in Joe McGinniss. It became possible to regard

*The Journalist and the Murderer* as obliquely confessional, and the same is true of *The Silent Woman.*

Malcolm leaves us in no doubt that *The Silent Woman* is a continuation by other means of the arguments put forth in *The Journalist and the Murderer.* Again she indicts an entire genre of literary production, and again she seems to be implicating herself—with whatever degree of ironic self-awareness—in the indictment. Biography's essential nature is "transgressive," she writes, and the biographer resembles a crook: not a con artist this time but a "professional burglar, breaking into a house, rifling through certain drawers that he has good reason to think contain the jewelry and money, and triumphantly bearing his loot away." Changing metaphors, she depicts biography and journalism as related pathologies, "virulent" strains of "the bacillus of bad faith," to which she is herself "susceptible."

Sylvia Plath's life and death have become a cherished feminist myth, and the imperatives of biographers seeking to perpetuate it are usually given priority over the keepers of the estate, jealous of their privacy and eager to put their own spin on destiny. Malcolm, the contrarian, sides with Ted Hughes and his protective older sister Olwyn, whose resistance to the biographical incursion may well be imagined; in the Plath legend, Hughes has always figured as the villain who hastened her demise. Malcolm prefers to see Hughes as Vronsky to Plath's Anna. The fact that Assia Wevill, the woman for whom Hughes left Plath, committed suicide in 1969, gassing herself as Plath had done "in a bizarre gesture of imitation," has the perhaps surprising effect of enlarging Malcolm's sympathy for the reclusive Hughes, Britain's current Poet Laureate.

In an allegory, everyone stands for something, and Hughes is the embattled artist: "His effort to disentangle his life from the Plath legend while tending its flame is a kind of grotesque allegory of the effort of every artist to salvage a piece of normal life for himself from the disaster of his calling." Olwyn Hughes is the "Cerberus" of the Plath estate. The cluttered-up house of a fatuous old man, whose claim to fame is that he dwelled in the flat below the one in which Plath took her life, becomes a "monstrous allegory of truth": "This is the way things are, the place says. This is unmediated actuality, in all its multiplicity, randomness, inconsistency, redundancy, *authenticity*. Before the magisterial mess of Trevor Thomas's house, the orderly houses that most of us live in seem meagre and lifeless—as, in the same way, the narratives called biographies pale and shrink in the face of the disorderly actuality that is a life."

There is more intellectual excitement in one of Malcolm's riffs than in many a thick academic tome. Consider her contention that "the nineteenth century came to an end in America only in the 1960s." Or this take on journalism: "The freedom to be cruel is one of journalism's uncontested privileges, and the rendering of subjects as if they were characters in bad novels is one of its widely accepted conventions."

Sometimes Malcolm goes too far, even for me—and I'm a big fan. There is, for example, the kitchen episode with Anne Stevenson, whose biography of Plath, *Bitter Fame*, was widely thought to have failed because she had made too many concessions to Olwyn Hughes. When Malcolm visited her in England, Stevenson prepared a lasagna dinner, forgetting at the last minute to insert an inessential ingredient ("the white sauce"). Here is how Malcolm magnifies the omission: "When we ate it, half an hour later, it tasted good, but Anne was critical of it and repeatedly apologized for it. As with the publication of *Bitter Fame*, she had no choice but to serve it, but she felt it to be an imperfect, compromised thing. I understood her anguish and felt for her." Turning Stevenson's hospitality into a homely metaphor for a failed literary enterprise seems both unfair and unkind, the sort of journalistic stunt that Malcolm deplores when she spots it in the work of others.

Malcolm raises ethical questions that almost all nonfiction writers must confront, and the fact that her own practices have been questioned scarcely invalidates her thesis or her individual insights. Summing up her own ambivalence, she likens herself to "a lawyer defending a case he knows to be weak and yet obscurely feels is just," but she is also the quavering defendant and the severe magistrate. When she condemns biography as a form of "voyeurism and busybodyism" that can be sadistic and cruel, what she is really doing is initiating a powerful argument with herself, for she knows that she shall not 'scape whipping. If *The Silent Woman* may be likened to a poem, it is not only because the writing is so fine but because of the truth in William Butler Yeats's observation that we make rhetoric out of our quarrels with others—and poetry out of our quarrels with ourselves.

# Over Their Dead Bodies

Raymond Chandler once remarked that the English may not be the best prose writers in the world but they are unquestionably the best *dull* prose writers in the world. I thought of this statement from time to time while reading Ian Hamilton's *Keepers of the Flame: Literary Estates and the Rise of Biography.* It is a good, dull book—factual, solid, well-researched—about a hot subject, the ethics of literary biography, and it has its share of juicy anecdotes. It is Hamilton's misfortune, however, that his study of professional widows, executors, and caretakers of literary estates should appear in the same season as Janet Malcolm's extraordinary book, *The Silent Woman: Sylvia Plath and Ted Hughes,* which raises similar issues but treats them in a manner that no one could call dull.

Malcolm's meditation on the enmity between Plath's widower and her hagiographers is everything Hamilton's book is not. He strives always to give the appearance of objectivity; she is highly subjective, frankly personal, deeply egocentric. She deals with the progress of one writer's posthumous reputation; he offers more than a dozen British cases, ranging from John Donne to Thomas Hardy, concluding with a chapter on Sylvia Plath and Philip Larkin, whose scandalous letters and life were last season's talk of the town. Hamilton's prose is serviceable, journalistic; the donnish one-liner is the rhetorical touch he favors (speaking of John Gibson Lockhart's life of Sir Walter Scott, he observes, for example, that "the prestige of the biography has kept pace with the prestige of its subject: just as Scott wrote far too much, so his biography is far too long").

---

Reviewed for the *New York Times Book Review,* March 27, 1994.

The irony is that Hamilton's book is allegorically about himself and his own literary predicaments, just as Malcolm's is about herself and hers. The case of Hamilton may be less fresh in people's minds, but it wasn't long ago that he was the outrage of the literary community, or that portion of it that is concerned with biography. Hamilton, the would-be biographer of J. D. Salinger who wouldn't take no for an answer, was sued by the reclusive author of *The Catcher in the Rye* for quoting his letters without permission. When the court decision went against Hamilton, it seemed to set a dangerous precedent.

Hamilton sounds a contrite note in the foreword to *Keepers of the Flame:* "It seems to me that fifty years is not too long for us to wait for the 'whole truth' about a private life," he writes, adding that "this may sound fishy" coming from "the near, would-be or failed biographer of J. D. Salinger." He's right; it does sound fishy. So far as I can see the stated position is not developed but belied in the pages that follow, in which Hamilton seems to be squarely on the side of the biographer. For Hamilton, who wrote a well-received life of Robert Lowell in addition to his book about Salinger, the heroic biographer is the truthteller going up against the masters of deception and spin control out to protect the reputation of great authors whose works may have been in better taste than their private lives.

As Hamilton demonstrates, the keepers of the flame of a great author's reputation often act out of selfish or ignoble motives, and sometimes the truth gets doctored in the process. Andrew Marvell's landlady, pretending to be his wife, published his poems as a legal ploy, "a means of declaring her entitlement" to funds from the Marvell estate. Vanity was the motive for John Cam Hobhouse, Byron's literary executor, who supervised the burning of a four-hundred-page memoir that Byron wrote; it is likely that Hobhouse, who wanted "to be acknowledged not just as Byron's friend but as his *best* friend," encountered something in the memoir that threatened this fond illusion. Prudery, too, can be a potent motive. The widows of Rudyard Kipling and Robert Louis Stevenson worked to sanitize their husbands' lives, suppressing roguish details; Rupert Brooke's mother made his biographer miserable.

Most authors leave it to their spouses and heirs to deal with their future biographers, but, as Mr. Hamilton tells us, Thomas Hardy took matters into his own hands. He wrote his own biography for publication under his wife's name after his death. No more illustrious (or less disinterested) a ghost writer ever toiled. After his death, his widow arranged to publish the manuscript as he wished, except that she excised almost all the favorable references to Hardy's first wife.

As a result of the obstructionism of an author's heirs, the life of Shelley is lost in a farrago of forged epistles, aborted biographies, and whitewashing pseudomemoirs. Was Shelley a sinner and a cad or an ineffectual angel beating in the void his luminous wings? We'll never know. We'll never know whether the glamorous romantic poet's face was notable for "firmness and hardness" or for its "feminine" cast, since accounts differ on even these details. "Small wonder," Hamilton comments, "that Shelley's son took up photography."

These are first-rate stories, and Hamilton presents them intelligently. He even states some of the major theoretical issues involved. For example, "the old insolubles: does poetic genius excuse or mitigate bad conduct; does/should knowing about the life have a bearing on how we read the work?" And there are other insolubles as well: when does the biographical imperative—and just what is that, exactly—justify "contempt for old habits of decorum and respectfulness"? But Hamilton neglects to argue out the irreconcilable conflicts that face the biographer; he stands at a polite distance, though his own experience has involved him deeply in these very issues. *Keepers of the Flame* works as a sequence of chapters loosely linked by theme but without a provocative central thesis. American readers expect more excitement. English majors—from traditional regiments, at any rate—may enjoy the book nevertheless.

# Literal Lives

Lamb wrote a dissertation on roast pig.
Hogg and Suckling did not. Wordsworth
Was not what you would call an economical writer.
Wilde tamed London. Pater was his literary father.

Pound earned a small but steady income from his writ-
     ing.
Ping-pong was Tennyson's favorite indoor sport.
No one else had done what Donne did in verse:
Erotic lyrics in a religious idiom, and vice-versa.

Racine's roots went deep into France's classical soil.
*The Iliad* was Homer's first grand slam.
*The Spanish Tragedy* exemplifies Kyd's mature style.
Swift wrote slowly. Pope pontificated.

Frost wondered whether the world would end in ice.
Moore was less wordy than Longfellow, whose short
     poems
Are his best. Peacock strutted. Bishop
Preferred Rio to Rome and the Vatican.

Ford couldn't drive a car. Neither, of course, could
Austen. As a child Woolf adored the story of
Little red riding hood. West died in California.
Mann loved women. Hardy endured.

*New Republic,* December 18, 1989.

# Philip Larkin's Letters

When he died at age sixty-three in 1985, Philip Larkin was properly regarded as the finest poet Britain had produced in the years since World War II. Though he wrote few poems and published fewer, did nothing to cultivate an American audience, and was about as politically incorrect as a white heterosexual male could be, readers on both sides of the Atlantic memorized his words, got a kick out of his opinions, and held the poet himself (as they imagined him to be) in affectionate regard. It was never any secret that the reclusive author was a reactionary and a xenophobe, a fussy bachelor, a blocked writer, misanthropic, provincial, sour, profane, and full of base prejudices.

Despite his Oxford degree (with honors) and the adulation and acclaim that were his during the last thirty years of his life, Larkin opted to go to Hull, toiling as a librarian at that distant northern university far from literary London. Mistrustful of the modern world and all its devices, he loved pre-bop jazz, poetry in the plain style, and little else; he managed to avoid owning a television set until he was fifty-seven, by which time he was deaf—his deafness a textbook example of a mental inclination given physical form. Shutting out the noise of the world, drinking himself to a nightly oblivion, Larkin could easily have turned into a professional crank if not for his marvelous talent for a poetry of pathos and astringent wit.

The self in Larkin's work was self-doubting, anti-heroic, prematurely middle-aged from the start. "Sad Steps"—the

Review of *Selected Letters of Philip Larkin 1940–1985*, ed. Anthony Thwaite. *Boston Globe,* December 12, 1993.

title a nod to Sir Philip Sidney's famous sonnet about the moon—enacts the characteristic Larkin movement: the poem may culminate in lines that capture the poignancy of lost youth but it begins very deliberately with the poet "groping back to bed after a piss" at four in the morning. Elsewhere he recorded the frustrations of bachelorhood with a certain dry humor. In, for example, "Annus Mirabilis": "Sexual intercourse began / In nineteen sixty-three / (Which was rather late for me)— / Between the end of the *Chatterley* ban / And the Beatles' first LP."

Larkin's poems are full of desolate attics, empty streets, inaccessible girls mounted in a photograph album, awkward men in trousers cinched with cycle clips, who want to make a dramatic gesture—to clear out, take off, leave everything behind—but can't quite muster up the gumption to decline an invitation to a party with "a crowd of craps." Above all, Larkin mastered the accents of sadness, a tone suitable to the imperial lion in decline, a life of little defeats and big mysteries, unhappiness and the fear of death: "Most things may never happen: this one will."

The irascible personality discreetly on view in Larkin's four slender volumes of verse is writ obnoxiously large in the thick tome of his letters. Larkin was as gabby in private as he was reticent in public. With their gratuitous slurs (Italy is "Wopland," and the poet Vikram Seth has produced a "load of crap," which "comes of being an oriental"), their calculated nastiness (he corresponds amiably with Anthony Powell, who becomes a "horse-faced dwarf" behind his back), and schoolboy crudeness (turning Emily Dickinson into "Emily Prick-in-son," or spewing out invective against unnamed "sodding loudmouthed cunting shitstuffed pisswashed sons of poxed-up bitches"), Larkin's letters are far from incongruous.

On the contrary, Larkin's epistolary life is continuous with poems that dismiss books generically as a "load of crap." The Larkin of the letters is recognizably the author of "Posterity," a short poem satirizing Jake Balokowsy, imaginary American Semite and academic hack, who makes Larkin his ticket to tenure. The poem's anti-Semitism stinks, though it should be noted that Larkin, never one to exempt himself from his strictures, lets Balokowsky have the last word. He sums up his creator as an "old fart"—"One of those old-type *natural* fouled-up guys."

Larkin's letters caused a major flap when they were published in England because what amuses in selected bits becomes insupportable in bulk—and because for the most part the letters, valuable and fascinating as they are, lack the literary excuse the poems make for the foul-mouthed lad who pops up in them. It is true that the most indulgent reader will sometimes shake his head reading these pages. The clever cracks ("Good old Graham, always the saham," Larkin says of Graham Greene's novels) are outweighed by the tasteless ones ("Keep up the cracks about niggers and wogs"). Whatever the opposite of a "class act" is, it is perfectly illustrated when Larkin, juggling mistresses, confides in one of them that he wishes he "had some of the money back" he had spent on the other, "*and the time*" [italics his].

Most people who think they have no illusions have at least that one. Of disillusioned ex-romantics, Larkin is less deceived than most. Knowing himself to be more sinning than sinned against, he owned up to being "a self-centered person conducting an affair containing no responsibilities with one girl getting mixed up with another, heedless of the feelings of either." This unusual lucidity may not excuse bad behavior. But politically correct critics fail to discriminate between person and persona, and one feels one should temper one's disapproval with the knowledge that Larkin is at his lewdest and most unbecoming in correspondence with his closest, indeed lifelong friends, the writers Kingsley Amis and Robert Conquest, with whom he is consciously posturing, delighting in being naughty—to the end of his life the ex-Oxonian who missed his pals because now there was no one with whom he could utter forbidden words.

Larkin's letters chronicle the process by which he turned almost self-consciously into a caricature. But a more fascinating drama also unfolds in these pages, the poignant Jamesian drama of a man obsessed with the fear that he will be the man to whom nothing will happen. Larkin turns into this character before our eyes, turning down all opportunities—and there are enough of them—to embark on an adventure or to celebrate his freedom. He is always saying no—to the chance of holding the university chair of poetry at Oxford in 1973 (he had W. H. Auden's vote); to the offer of an exclusive reviewing arrangement with the London *Observer;* to the invitation to bring out a revised edition of his controversial anthology, *The Oxford Book of Twentieth Century English Verse;* and finally, when his friend Sir John Betjeman died in 1984, to the royal appointment as England's Poet Laureate.

As the letters more than even the poems demonstrate, Larkin's was the drama of a fearful man, frightened of life, of risk, of change. Marriage terrified him. Women made him "rigid with fright," he tells a boyhood friend. He was shy of thirty when he withdrew "a garbled proposal of marriage" from a long-term fiancée. He out-Prufrocked Prufrock: "Sufficient for me to choose something to dislike it," he confesses. "If we part I shall be tormented by remorse at not having married. If we marry I shall spend my life mentally kicking myself for having so carelessly given up priceless liberty." The hell of marriage was worse then the Hull of loneliness, he decided. "A happy marriage," he declared flatly thirty years on, is "a contradiction in terms."

In time his fear attached itself at last to an object commensurate in size and scope with its intensity. The fear of death is the theme of Larkin's strongest poems, such as the magnificent "Aubade" (1977), the one poem he turned out in the barren last decade of his life: "Courage is no good: / It means not scaring others. Being brave / Lets no one off the grave. / Death is no different whined at than withstood."

Larkin's case of writer's block grew to become the immovable rock blocking the cave mouth. Why? In part, I think, because the very stance on which his poems were predicated was one of determined failure. His was a poetry of limited scope and reduced expectation. It wouldn't do to be prolific in such circumstances—it would be like making too much noise about silence. Larkin practiced a strict poetics of sincerity, refusing to write except when inspiration and need converged. He made things harder for himself by categorically rejecting modernism, experimentalism, and the myriad paths they offer.

Larkin felt that Charlie Parker was the death of jazz, the equivalent of Picasso in painting and Ezra Pound in poetry. There are many in and out of the jazz world who would regard the analogy as a compliment. But for Larkin—who wrote a quirky book on the subject—improvisational jazz that left the melody behind was anathema, as were the painterly movements that shattered the object (cubism) or erased it (abstract expressionism). Maybe the most poignant phrase in this book occurs in an otherwise sour letter Larkin wrote in 1963: "I used to be fond of jazz."

Here is a Larkin sampler culled from the letters. "Literature is a very tiny thing compared with one's own life." "As always when you are out of reach I am amazed by my good fortune that you were ever within it." "Autumn and winter are better than spring and summer in that they are not supposed to be enjoyable." "Personally I should need only two words to describe English poetry since 1960 ('horse-shit')." "My mind has stopped at 1945, like some cheap wartime clock." "I never buy anything but petrol and drink." "What I like about Phil, he always cheers you up." "Life has nothing to offer after fifty, and after sixty doesn't bear thinking about."

In the end, the epithets, the put-downs, the glee taken in spank magazines, and so forth, are not really very shocking, or not shocking in a way that would detract from our pleasure in the poems. Larkin's story was always more conducive to sorrow than to anger. He was the poet whom youth abandoned too soon. He lost his hair, gained a paunch, drank too much in private, and became "one of those old-type *natural* fouled-up guys." He wrote too little, but his best work had an eloquence altogether convincing, because all the grand wild glib romantic gestures had been so assiduously eschewed. I would sooner read Larkin than any of his contemporaries in Britain. That hasn't changed.

# Frank O'Hara's Life

Among the vanguard poets of his generation, Frank O'Hara (1926–1966) had a singularly liberating influence on younger writers. What he called his "I do this I do that" poems—peripatetic chronicles of his casual movements and thoughts—were like a great permission slip, an emancipation from the yoke of T. S. Eliot's academic epigones.

O'Hara, as Brad Gooch writes in *City Poet: The Life and Times of Frank O'Hara,* was "refreshingly modern," a metropolitan poet in a jacket and windblown tie shuttling from "an enormously demanding day job"—he was a curator at the Museum of Modern Art—to a hyperactive "downtown" existence in an era when it actually meant something to be avant-garde. Full of art galleries and painters' lofts, French cigarettes and Italian liqueurs, O'Hara's poems made poetry seem as natural as breathing, as sexy as jazz. They made it seem the height of glamour to be a poet in New York City in the fifties and early sixties.

O'Hara had a particular talent for "playing the typewriter," whether or not a party was going on at the time; he liked composing on the run, living in the heart of noise. He dashed off numerous poems on his lunch break, and on one memorable occasion broke up an audience—and showed up Robert Lowell, with whom he was sharing the podium—by reading the hilarious poem he had written on his way to the gathering. ("I was in such a hurry / to meet you but the traffic / was acting

Review of *City Poet: The Life and Times of Frank O'Hara,* by Brad Gooch. Published as "A Poet in the Heart of Noise" in *New York Times Book Review,* June 20, 1993.

exactly like the sky / and suddenly I see a headline / LANA TURNER HAS COLLAPSED!")

Feeling that poems could be as immediate and spontaneous as phone calls, O'Hara developed an improvisatory style capable of recording a "meditation in an emergency" or a reverie triggered by the glimpsed headline of an afternoon paper. A *New York Post* with Billie Holiday's picture on it occasioned "The Day Lady Died," perhaps his most famous poem, which moves from the particulars of train schedules and errands to this breathless climax:

> and I am sweating a lot by now and thinking of
> leaning on the john door in the 5 SPOT
> while she whispered a song along the keyboard
> to Mal Waldron and everyone and I stopped breathing

Gregarious and seemingly indefatigable, capable of great charm and a marvelously bitchy wit, O'Hara had what many artists lack—the capacity to enjoy the work of others—and he had it to the nth degree. His combination of limitless enthusiasm and instinctive good taste was hard to resist.

At O'Hara's funeral, the painter Larry Rivers said, "There are at least sixty people in New York who thought Frank O'Hara was their best friend," a number that kept growing after his death. He was unquestionably the pivotal figure in the New York School of poetry, whose other charter members included John Ashbery, Kenneth Koch, and James Schuyler. But only O'Hara in that group of best friends celebrated city and self in the style of Walt Whitman. The very rhythms of New York enact themselves in his lines, the horns honking, the heels clicking.

Mr. Gooch gives a full account of the freak accident that slit his subject's thin-spun life at the age of forty in July 1966. After a Saturday night spent drinking with buddies, O'Hara was run over at about 2:40 in the morning by a joy-riding Jeep on a Fire Island beach, where there isn't supposed to be any traffic. The beach buggy he'd been riding in had broken down, and he had wandered off tipsily in the dark to look at the ocean while waiting for a replacement vehicle to get there.

He might have survived the collision, but his liver was shot from all the days he had begun with vodka and grapefruit juice or bourbon and soda. Mr. Gooch suggests he had been all but burned out for the two years preceding his death.

Before reading *City Poet,* I hadn't realized the intensity of the sadness at the core of O'Hara's being, and I am still not fully able to account for it. Born in Baltimore, where his parents lived for eighteen months to conceal the illegitimacy of his birth, O'Hara rebelled against the Irish Catholicism of family and parochial school in Grafton, Massachusetts, where he grew up. The Navy in the closing months of World War II was one ticket out; Harvard, which O'Hara attended on the G.I. Bill, was another. In Cambridge he roomed with the artist Edward Gorey and published stories and poems in *The Harvard Advocate;* while in graduate school at the University of Michigan, he wrote for Cambridge's newly formed Poets' Theater. In New York he came into his own not only as a writer but as a catalyst for the creativity of others.

Various women, including the painters Jane Freilicher and Grace Hartigan, took turns as O'Hara's muse, but the loves of his life were strictly male. Like his mother, whom he grew to detest, he had a terminal drinking problem, though his productivity and high energy disguised the fact. "For a creative, ambitious alcoholic," remarked a friend, "he was a perfect role model." Morbidly affected by the deaths of other artists, O'Hara wrote elegies for James Dean and was convinced that he, too, would die young. Once, in a game of Twenty Questions, somebody asked him what he was most afraid of. "Living beyond forty," he answered.

Though enjoyable and easy to read, *City Poet* has a major flaw. The nice way of putting it is that the book is free of pretension. The frank way is to say that it is relentlessly superficial. To declare, for example, that "the poets of the New York School could be grouped together because they wrote in language that was illogical and often meaningless" is an inexcusably reductive statement in a biography of Frank O'Hara.

Painlessly turning pages, the reader doesn't come away with a clear idea of why O'Hara was so original a voice and so beloved a figure. Nor do we ever really get a sense of what made him tick—or drove him to drink. It is a bit disconcerting to discover that O'Hara's mother has gone, in Mr. Gooch's portrait, from a nurturer to a witch without much explanation.

O'Hara's literary friendships fare little better. Mr. Gooch (himself a novelist and poet whose work shows the influence of the New York School) refers to the "deeply affectionate" yet "competitive" nature of O'Hara's friendship with John Ashbery. O'Hara likened the pair to the brothers in *East of Eden*, identifying himself with the James Dean figure while suggesting that Ashbery was "full of dreams and a kind of moral excellence."

The two poets competed for the same prizes, compared notes on the same films and books, and when they attended a concert of John Cage's "Music for Changes" on New Year's Day, 1952, Ashbery reported that he had a major breakthrough in his work.

John Ashbery went to Paris in 1955, and the friends were separated for most of the following ten years. In March 1960, right in the middle of that period, O'Hara flew to Madrid to scout out paintings for an exhibition he was mounting at the Museum of Modern Art; Ashbery joined him there, and the two spent the next three weeks in close quarters, proceeding to Barcelona, San Sebastian, Biarritz, and Paris. Yet Mr. Gooch—attentive as ever to O'Hara's love interest of the moment (a dancer in New York)—scarcely has a word on what O'Hara talked about, did, and saw with Ashbery during their time together. The close and complicated friendship of these two remarkable poets is one of a number of subjects that deserve a more considered treatment than they get in *City Poet*.

# Old Man Rivers

Larry Rivers's life is as colorful as the spectacularly original canvases that have firmly established his place among the major avant-garde artists of our time. Born Yitzroch Grossberg in the Bronx, Rivers was an uninhibited, grass-smoking, sex-obsessed jazz saxophonist in his early twenties when he picked up a paintbrush for the first time. The year was 1945; the war was about to end, and New York City was on the cusp of becoming the art capital of the world.

Encouraged by such estimable painters as Jane Freilicher and Nell Blaine, Rivers soon "began thinking that art was an activity on a 'higher level' than jazz," because music is "abstract" and can't be done alone whereas painting is a solo performance that allows the artist to "make nameable things." Rivers took drawing classes with the great Hans Hofmann, but he always retained the improvisatory ideal of jazz, and the make-it-up-as-you-go-along approach has served him well. Even his most monumental constructions, such as *The History of the Russian Revolution* (1965) in Washington's Hirshhorn Museum, have a fresh air of spontaneity about them, as if they had been assembled just a few minutes ago.

Rivers had a meteoric rise. A Pierre Bonnard exhibition at New York's Museum of Modern Art in 1948 proved to have a decisive influence on his sense of color and composition. No less an eminence than Clement Greenberg, then the nation's foremost art critic, declared in 1949 that Rivers was already "a

Review of *What Did I Do? The Unauthorized Autobiography of Larry Rivers,* by Larry Rivers with Arnold Weinstein, published in the *Washington Post Book World,* December 27, 1992.

better composer of pictures than was Bonnard himself in many instances"—and this on the basis of Rivers's first one-man show. Though Greenberg would later modify his praise and then withdraw it altogether, he had launched the career of "this amazing beginner."

If one condition of avant-garde art is that it is ahead of its time and another is that it proceeds from a maverick impulse and a contrary disposition, Rivers's vanguard status was assured from the moment when, at the height of abstract expressionism, he audaciously made representational paintings, glorifying nostalgia and sentiment while undercutting them with metropolitan irony. His pastiches of famous paintings of the past—such as his irreverent rendition of *Washington Crossing the Delaware* (1953)—seemed to define the playfully ironic attitudes of postmodernism years before anyone had thought up that term. And his paintings of brand labels, found objects, and pop icons—Camel cigarettes, Dutch Masters cigars, the menu at the Cedar Bar in 1959, a French hundred-franc note—demonstrate what is vital about Pop Art while escaping the limitations of that movement.

Rivers has his own style of painting: he relies on "charcoal drawing and rag wiping." Also distinctive is his prankish sense of humor. In 1964 he painted a spoof of Jacques-Louis David's famous *Napoleon in His Study*, the portrait of the emperor in the classic hand-in-jacket pose. Rivers's version, full of smudges and erasures, manages to be iconoclastic and idolatrous at once. The finishing touch is the painting's title: Rivers called it *The Greatest Homosexual*.

*What Did I Do?*, Rivers's autobiographical ramble, conveys the excitement, the nervous energy, and the sublime agitation of life in New York City at a time when rents were cheap, Lester Young was president of the republic of jazz, and painters of the caliber of Willem de Kooning and Franz Kline hung out at the Cedar Bar, which thus became, in Rivers's phrase, "the G-spot of the art scene." Obsessed with "art and the quest for sex," Rivers left his wife for the floating bohemia of Manhattan, where he shot up heroin, was openly bisexual, and lived with his two sons and his mother-in-law, Berdie, whom he painted—sometimes in the nude.

Rivers had (and has) an adventuresome spirit, an appetite for notoriety, and a nose for publicity. He won a lot of money on "The $64,000 Challenge," one of the fixed TV game shows of the fifties, until he met his Waterloo when he was asked to identify the maiden name of Renoir's wife. Later, Rivers made the most of his opportunity to testify at a grand jury investigation of the program, acting as if the courtroom were an extension of show biz by other means. One of the show's producers, Rivers tells us, was his friend Shirley Bernstein, "sister of Lenny." When Rivers denied that she had fed him the answers, the assistant district attorney fired back, "Why are you protecting her, Mr. Rivers?" In response, Rivers writes, he "rose from the witness chair and said dramatically, 'Because I love her—and I don't care if the whole world knows it!' "

Long on anecdote, short on analysis, *What Did I Do?* is full of juicy stories about Rivers's friends and associates, and he seems to have been chums with aesthetic experimentalists of all stripes, from the Living Theatre's Julian Beck and Judith Malina ("violent pacifists," Rivers calls them) to John Cage (whose music "was like a sermon by Spike Jones"), Jasper Johns and Robert Rauschenberg, not to mention the poets of the New York School, with whom Rivers became fast friends: Frank O'Hara, Kenneth Koch, John Ashbery, James Schuyler, Harry Mathews. He and O'Hara ("a charming madman") were intermittently lovers. They collaborated on several inspired projects, such as a hilarious send-up of an art manifesto, "How to Proceed in the Arts": "How can we paint the elephants and the hippopotamuses? How are we to fill the large empty canvas at the end of the large empty loft? You do have a loft, don't you, man?"

Rivers is a world-class talker, and reading *What Did I Do?* is like listening to a candid, manic monologue. It is an experiment in discontinuous narrative, with frequent flashbacks and flashforwards, and it is an awful lot of fun. It isn't always easy to piece together the chronology—Rivers places his trust in memory, that least reliable of fact-checkers—but that isn't the point. The real subject of this book, and its greatest pleasure, is the personality of the artist: mercurial, profane, madcap, somewhat exhibitionistic, sometimes puerile: a wiseguy who gets a kick out of shocking the censor.

In the book's preface, Rivers introduces us to his collaborator on this project, the writer Arnold Weinstein: "I knew the three women he married, he probably fucked both my wives. What can I say? He's an old pal." That is the authentic Rivers tone, and it spices up every page. Some of his riffs are extraordinary. One of his sons is "deranged but normal in every other way." Rivers and his second wife, Clarice, "parted in 1967 and have been married ever since." Or consider this echo of the book's title: "For someone who has always had fantasies of living in a whorehouse like my heroes Pascin, Lautrec, Van Gogh, and Utamaro, what am I doing with five children, adding up to 252 pairs of shoes, 1,008 boxes of cereal, hot and cold, 8,660 quarts of milk, etc., plus 23 analysts, including mine?"

# James Merrill: Another Life

James Merrill is a lyric poet with a novelist's agenda. Elegant, graceful, puckish, lithe, he has steadily put his sonnets and intricate stanzas at the service of autobiographical themes and narrative ends. With rare candor and rarer tact Merrill has explored the broken home of his childhood, the romance of art and myth and dreams and travel, his aestheticism, his homosexuality, and the whole rich gamut of experiences available to a man who was always spared the financial angst that plagues most poets.

Merrill, the scion of a large fortune, had different problems. As a nine-year-old rich boy in New York he was afraid of being abducted, as the Lindbergh baby was. But he imagined that he would come to love his captors, gangster Floyd and his moll Jean, preferring them to his parents: the fantasy that gets played out in Merrill's "Days of 1935" in his collection *Braving the Elements* (1972).

The surprise in Merrill's career came about as a result of his infatuation with the Ouija board. A thousand and one nights spent conjuring up spirits familiar and strange led him to construct an epic poem of major proportions. Comprising three books and an epilogue, and running over 17,000 lines, *The Changing Light at Sandover* (1983) presents a vision of the afterlife with a structure derived from Dante's *Divine Comedy* and with similarly cosmic ambitions, but with all the insouciance of a reveler at the Mad Hatter's tea party.

---

Review of *A Different Person: A Memoir,* by James Merrill, in the *Washington Post Book World,* September 12, 1993.

A year ago Merrill's publisher reissued *Sandover* along with an enlarged edition of his *Selected Poems*. Rereading the former, one is struck anew by how marvelously he manages to mix lofty and low elements, proving that a poem of the highest seriousness may cheerfully make do with the stage machinery of sci-fi novels, operatic high-tech phantasmagoria, and genteel spiritualism of the sort that Noel Coward sent up in *Blithe Spirit.*

Merrill's latest offering is a book of prose—his best book of prose to date. (He is also the author of several novels and a miscellany of critical pieces and short stories.) *A Different Person* is a highly unusual and compelling example of a genre that has been flourishing of late, the personal memoir. Beautifully written, with insights into love and passion that place the poet in the company of Benjamin Constant and Stendhal, the book tells the story of the two and a half years Merrill spent in Europe as a young man in his twenties. But it is not a mere impressionistic record; Merrill uses the European sojourn as an organizing convenience, a narrative center. His aim here, as in his poems, is to know himself— to come to terms with his experiences, self-critically but with his vast capacity for puzzlement and wonder—and, in the process, to chart out the growth of a poet's mind.

The young poet had studied at Amherst, had taught at Bard, and was floundering about, full of anxieties and sensibility, when he sailed to Europe in 1950 in search of his Jamesian destiny. He knew he would eventually come back, and that when he did he would be a different person—changed by his love affairs in Paris, his psychoanalysis in Rome, his deepening passion for the opera, his difficult relations with his father (Charles Merrill of Merrill Lynch) and his dowager mother. He is terribly unsure of himself on page one, afraid of being alone, a good candidate for the writer's block that will indeed afflict him in Europe; by the book's conclusion, we have come in contact with the person who will write the poems.

In *Sandover*, Merrill alternated between upper- and lowercase type, using the former to record the sayings of his heavenly informants; typography reinforced the book's vision of an angelic hierarchy. Here, too, the typesetting makes a real difference. In *A Different Person* Merrill alternates between roman and italic type to distinguish time past from time present, the time of the action from the time of composition. The story of the European sojourn is told in roman—suitably, since the eternal city is a prime locale—with italic type reserved for the chapter-ending passages in which the poet comments from the vantage point of forty years on.

Merrill's title yields multiple meanings. Every young man, studied by himself with sixty winters on his head, is a different person in the sense of L. P. Hartley's immortal line: "The past is a foreign country. They do things differently there." But Merrill was always conscious of his difference from others— and from parental expectation. "From the age of nineteen I've been made to feel . . . my difference from the rest of the world, a difference laudable and literary at noon, shocking and sexual at midnight," he writes. His mother strongly disapproved of his homosexuality, and some of the most moving pages in this book are devoted to the poet's continuing dialogues with her, some actual, some imaginary.

Merrill, whose affinity for Proust has often been noted, is a philosopher of love in the French tradition. He gives us, for example, "that curious but widespread law whereby people instinctively withhold what you want from them." In an extraordinary passage he wonders about his father's habit of maintaining warm relations with ex-spouses—his unwillingness to break with past amours. Recognizing the same tendency in himself, the poet suddenly feels "the pain my father must have caused his latest love by never quite relinquishing the bygone ones."

Merrill's prose style is nacreous, with some of the finest pearls concealed in subordinate phrases and incidental figures of speech. His writing is full of inspired plays on words ("the Spanish steps uplifted their descender") and ingenious similes ("His manners were natural, even humble, like the hut of forest boughs that shelter a great wizard"). Inveterate lover of opera that he is, Merrill regularly breaks the recitative of his life to launch an aria of reflection or heightened emotion.

An acquaintance of the poet, an Italian count, has arranged a visit to Sansepolcro, where Merrill sets eyes on Piero della Francesca's magnificent *Resurrection*. The painting triggers off a passage in which the vocation of the artist and the mission of Jesus Christ are brilliantly compared and contrasted:

> Deep down I feared that Jesus and I, both, had reached our zenith as children and that I would be hard put to avoid a terminal phase shot through, like his, by showmanship and self-promotion. Weren't those, however, among the traits I saw Jesus as sharing with the artists I most admired? Like Baudelaire he had a weakness for loose women. Like Mallarme he enthralled and mystified his disciples; like Oscar Wilde, courted ruin at the height of his fame. Like Proust he had dipped, with miraculous consequences, a cookie into a restorative cup. . . .

For admirers of Merrill's poetry *A Different Person* will be indispensable. In an aside, he attributes the difficulty of his early work to "the need to conceal my feelings, and their objects"; the pronoun *you* recommended itself to him because it was "genderless as a figleaf," thus concealing the writer's homosexuality.

Merrill has always relied on rituals and parlor games to generate the stuff of poetry. In *A Different Person* he gives us the directions for a "game of Murder": "Each player draws a slip of paper from a bowl and examines it secretly. All the slips are blank but for two—one marked with a black dot for the Murderer, the other with an X for the Cross-Examiner. In darkness the players wander from room to room." The murderer hopes to escape undetected when he deals "a gently stylized blow to the heart" of his chosen victim. Then the questioning begins.

It was Merrill's luck to receive the slip of paper with the big black dot on it when he played the game of Murder in Rome. Merrill's description of that party reminds us of the surprising affinities that exist between the rules of a game and those of a literary composition—as between a love affair and a crime of the heart.

# An Unsentimental Education

The personal memoir as a literary form has never had it so good. The fall lists of major publishing houses include autobiographical works by all manner of folk, from former British prime minister Margaret Thatcher to former *Harper's* editor Willie Morris, not to mention Hitler's filmmaker Leni Riefenstahl, New York intellectual Diana Trilling, poets Donald Hall and James Merrill, and actor Tony Curtis. Alice Kaplan's memoir *French Lessons* is unique in this company for the simple reason that, unlike the others, she is a writer in whose life most readers can have little interest except to the extent that her writing quickens it. Against the odds *French Lessons* succeeds admirably. Kaplan has written a far more satisfying book than, for example, Willie Morris's ballyhooed *New York Days,* with its sentimentalized evocation of the hip Manhattan literary scene in the late sixties.

Kaplan, thirty-eight, a professor of French at Duke University, is at that stage in her academic career when people begin to substitute "accomplished" for "promising" in describing her. A scholar specializing in the works of French fascist intellectuals, she is a veteran of graduate studies at Yale, a survivor of the reign of critical terrorism, who got her dose of deconstruction firsthand from Paul de Man himself. Her book is about the formation of her mind and the realization of her commitment to her professorial calling. It is like a classic *bildungsroman,* with the curious difference that the protagonist is not an artist contemplating the vocation of art but a critic contemplating her life and tenure.

---

*Los Angeles Times Book Review,* October 10, 1993.

Kaplan's success in *French Lessons* has to do with her invigorating prose—she has, as she puts it, a "staccato Midwestern style"—and with her unflinching honesty. Whether she is writing about personal experience or intellectual history, about the trauma of her first menstrual period or about the semiotic importance of Joan of Arc in contemporary French politics, she is lucid, succinct, matter-of-fact: three adjectives that rarely apply to professors of French literature, those prolix proponents of cutting-edge critical theories who never seem to have heard of Gallic clarity.

Kaplan writes affectingly about "the privilege of living in translation." She wants to know why she was so drawn to the study of French, and indeed one distinguishing trait of *French Lessons* is the urgency the writer brings to the task of understanding her own motivations. She writes about a teacher who made a difference at Berkeley, about the lessons she learned from her French boyfriend during her junior year abroad at Bordeaux, about the compulsion to pronounce the French "r" correctly and the self-abnegation needed to do so. In France, in French, she could be a different person, invent herself anew. French gave her, as she puts it, "a place to hide," but it was also "a sacred language," a storehouse of secrets, and a mask allowing the wearer to lead a life of pure duality, for which Kaplan has a penchant.

It has been said that if English is like a violin, French is like a piano, and a sonata for the two instruments should prove their incompatibility. Kaplan's ruminations about difference and discordance, the places where the self gets lost in translation, and the trials and terrors of an American woman striding on French intellectual turf, are memorable. She is a good teacher, making grammar come to life when, to illustrate the difference in nuance between the passé composé and the imperfect tense, she analyzes a passage in *The Stranger* by Albert Camus.

Activists in the resistance to deconstruction will take heart from *French Lessons,* citing the book as evidence of a return to history on the part of young American scholars. Deconstruction, as Kaplan puts it, was an elaboration of the insight that there is "something inherently deceitful about language." As exemplified in the impersonal ideal of Paul de Man, deconstruction was also "about keeping person-ness away." There were no characters in literature; they were all linguistic constructs, and language always lies. If you hunted hard enough for that place in any text where the language fatally undermines its own meaning-making power, you would find it. Eat the fruit of deconstruction and you would banish yourself from the realm of verifiable facts and knowable truths.

At a time when most of her colleagues were still working on rhetorical studies in the prescribed manner, describing linguistic circles in which they could chase their tails around the room, Kaplan chose the road not taken. She immersed herself in the study of that shameful period when enthusiastic French collaborationists welcomed the Nazis' new order, deporting French Jews and persecuting the French Resistance. That Kaplan, whose father was an attorney prosecuting Nazi war criminals at the Nuremberg trials, elected this scholarly course makes perfect sense—especially if you take into account the fact that Kaplan's father died when she was eight, and that much of her professional career may be defined as a search for a missing father.

This is the journey that she covers in *French Lessons*. It is a journey that required courage, nerve, and self-awareness, undertaken as it was before the train of deconstruction finally got derailed. What did it in was the shocking news that the revered de Man had written pro-Nazi propaganda in Europe during World War II. The immediate downtick in the fortunes of deconstruction was matched by the enhanced market value of an expert on French fascist aesthetics: Kaplan was in the right place at the right time and has prospered. Still, having had no inkling of de Man's fascist past until after his death, she will always regret that she never asked "the questions I could have asked him, had I known to ask." She is right to exclaim: "What a waste!"

Kaplan's rejection of deconstruction is far from unequivocal. Although she recognizes the self-serving applications of a critical theory that militates against truth, meaning, history, and personality, she insists that "deconstruction was good for us" in the sense that it spawned rigorous techniques for the close reading of texts. Well, maybe. But as one who regards deconstruction as an unmitigated academic disaster, I am bound to side with Guy, the author's ex-boyfriend from her Yale days. Kaplan reports that he criticized an essay she wrote on the de Man affair. He faults her for ending the essay with, in her own words, "impossibility and the confusion of theory and life" instead of taking a definite stand.

In *French Lessons*, Kaplan turns the tables on Guy, who had also studied with de Man. "God," Guy muses, "why did I always have the feeling he never talked to one." Her cool comment: "At the very moment when [Guy is] trying to say how angry he was that de Man had ignored him, he goes impersonal on his pronoun. Why, after all this time, couldn't he say, 'the man never really talked to me'?" Touché. Kaplan wants this episode to demonstrate the value of rhetorical analysis for the revelation of character. It may do that, but it also enables her to dodge—here, as in her earlier essay on the de Man affair—the more pertinent question raised by Guy: what part *did* de Man's wartime behavior play in the making of "the cool ironic theorist of language from whom we had tried to learn"?

Kaplan understands the need for factual accuracy but makes a couple of sloppy errors in her chapter on de Man. She reports the rumor that he "married the daughter of a U.S. Senator" but fails to make it clear that the rumor is false. He taught at Bard College, not Bennington, in the late forties. An article on the de Man scandal in *Newsweek,* not *Time,* provoked the correspondence with the Duke graduate student to which she refers. Small errors, granted: but disturbing in a book with a section entitled "Getting It Right."

Still, I like this book. I like its intelligence and passion, its candor, all of which helped me overcome my prejudice against memoirs written by people under the age of forty. Above all I like the author's willingness to put herself on the line. "Now I'm helping my own Ph.D. students write their dissertations, and I don't want to fail them the way that de Man failed me," she writes. "How do I tell them who I am, why I read the way I do? What do students need to know about their teachers?" *French Lessons* answers the need beautifully.

# The Case of Michel Foucault

For upwards of two decades in the United States, the academic study of literature and, increasingly, that of the humanities in general, has been under the sway of a band of formidably esoteric philosophers from Paris. The biggest names are those of Roland Barthes, Jacques Derrida, Michel Foucault, and Jacques Lacan, a diverse enough quartet in some respects but with a number of things in common, such as their vaguely Gallic insistence on there being a strong "erotic" dimension in activities not ordinarily considered sexual, like reading a book. And the purveyors of literary criticism and theory in the United States have borne out this proposition in a sense by allowing themselves to be seduced, compromised, and betrayed by these brilliant Frenchmen and the promise of liberation they seemed to proffer.

Foucault, who died of AIDS in 1984, was perhaps the most ambitious and the most disturbing of the lot. Only Derrida can rival Foucault in the depth and extent of his influence in the American academic world, and a comparison between them is instructive. Both men were influenced by German philosophers: in Derrida's case, Martin Heidegger; in Foucault's, Nietzsche. Both men are nihilistic, Derrida in a spirit of punmanship and play, Foucault in a darker, more visceral mode. What Derrida offered the world was deconstruction, an all-purpose neologism in whose name a great deal of double-talk has been unleashed. Foucault, by contrast, offered an obsessive concern with power—as if all

---

Review of *The Passion of Michel Foucault,* by James Miller, in the *Chicago Tribune,* February 21, 1993.

activities, whether in the bedroom or in jail, are allegories of power.

Knowledge is a function of power, Foucault argued, sparking a mini-industry of dissertations and term papers in which a system of hidden power relations is said to underlie a seemingly benevolent institution or convention. According to Foucault, knowledge is not something that has an independent, objective existence; knowledge is a construction, produced rather than discovered. What's more, it is the product not of consensus but of conflict. The "truth" depends on who has the power to enforce it. In *The Passion of Michel Foucault*, James Miller makes clear just how significant a line of thought this was and what appeal it exercised for a generation of American academics who came of age in the sixties.

Foucault translated Nietzsche's concept of the "will to power" into a philosophical imperative. This put him unequivocally against humanism, which he defined as "everything in Western civilization that restricts *the desire for power*" (Foucault's italics). Foucault worshipped at the shrine of death and Dionysus, glorified cruelty, and idealized the practices of sadomasochistic eroticism, as if one might effect a healthy transformation of the self by playing various parts in what Miller calls "an erotic theater of cruelty." For Foucault, crime was positive energy and the conscience was an agent not of moral rectitude but of perversion, alienating human beings from their true, cruel, animal natures.

*Discipline and Punish* (1975), Foucault's most important book, is a historical examination of criminal punishment and, as Miller says, "a seminal work of radical social criticism." It is also highly idiosyncratic. Comparing medieval torture and execution to the methods of modern prisons, Foucault comes out in favor of the former, because modern prison systems, with their emphasis on incarceration and surveillance, have in his view removed the terror, and thus the heroism, from the criminal life.

Foucault had an unrelenting fascination with the outcasts of society—the sick in hospitals, the inmates of asylums, prisoners in penitentiaries—and a penchant for using his personal life as an experimental laboratory for developing and testing his ideas. For Foucault, knowledge was to be acquired not as a set of concepts to be mastered but as a result of ordeals to be experienced. Searching for "limit-experiences"—a Foucauldian notion roughly equivalent to what Tom Wolfe means by "pushing the envelope"—the philosopher dropped acid in Death Valley and consumed great quantities of hashish. While a visiting professor at Berkeley, he frequented the gay bathhouses of San Francisco, particularly the ones specializing in "S/M." He regarded sex as a Faustian pact, judging it to be "worth dying for," and he refused to alter his behavior after the AIDS epidemic had broken out. There have been strong rumors to the effect that Foucault knowingly infected others with the disease. Miller's verdict: probably not. More likely, Foucault's unabated promiscuity was suicidal rather than murderous.

Like Miller's previous book, *Democracy in the Streets,* a lucid account of "the New Left" fashioned by college students of the sixties, *The Passion of Michel Foucault* is a valuable guide to treacherous intellectual terrain. It is clearly written and aims to be scrupulous and fair. If it is tougher going than *Democracy in the Streets,* that is because Foucault's thought—in theory and in practice—is more demanding, more difficult, and more dangerous than the thoughts of yesteryear's campus radicals.

Foucault's books, like those of the Marquis de Sade, are always stimulating. He contributed significantly to the assumption, now widespread, that marginal lives—like those of the prisoners and asylum residents he studied—may disclose central truths. He once pointed out that the fall of the Bastille in Paris in 1789, an event that is usually thought to have ignited the French Revolution, is undoubtedly a less important historical occurrence than, say, a change in the amount of protein in the average person's diet.

Miller tends to go a little too easy on Foucault. After explaining that Foucault thought that rape should be punishable only to the extent that it involved physical violence, Miller admits that "Foucault's specific proposals are highly questionable" and then hedges his bets by adding that "his courage" in maintaining that position "is beyond dispute." Still, he finds it hard to put a good face on Foucault's enthusiasm for the

Ayatollah Khomeini's Muslim revolution in Iran, an enthusiasm that only grew, says Miller, after the massacres in Teheran in September 1978.

Foucault dreamed of a "future society" at the end of a road paved by "drugs, sex, communes, [and] other forms of consciousness," and in retrospect, he looks as foolish (and as dated) as the campus utopians of the militant sixties and early seventies. It doesn't bother me to know that he was willing to jettison a project or alter a point of view as the result of an acid trip in the desert, but I can imagine that some of his more earnest followers may be put out by this example of his methods. Other aspects of Foucault's philosophy—such as his intellectual commitment to sadomasochism for its putative value in changing the self and redeeming the world—are even harder to countenance in the era of AIDS than they were during the innocence of the age of Aquarius.

Skeptical investigation of the sources of knowledge is Foucault's greatest intellectual legacy. Would that he had directed an equal amount of skepticism at the narcissistic, thrill-seeking self that demanded gratification even at the cost of its own annihilation.

# Part 4

# Criticism and Controversy

# Deconstruction after the Fall

## Signs and Designs

When I went to England for the British publication of *Signs of the Times* last fall, I gave a talk under the auspices of the Oxford University Literary Society. On selected walls and bulletin boards the organizers had hung posters identifying the guest speaker as "David Lehman, deconstructionist." Since deconstructionists frequently collapse the difference between a thing and its opposite, and since they and I are supposed to exist in a stage of mutual antipathy, I marveled at the poster. Surely, I thought, this was a sign of advanced irony in keeping with the elusive subject of my book. In line with the theories of Jacques Derrida and Paul de Man, the sign was perfectly undecidable—you couldn't tell from looking at it whether the identification of the speaker with deconstruction was based on a fundamental error or on sly wit.

In *Signs of the Times,* I set out to turn the tables on a table-turning theory—to deconstruct deconstruction, deride Derrida, and demand that de Man be held accountable for the words he had written for the Nazi-controlled press in his native Belgium during World War II. Did the sign on the wall signify that I was somehow in league with deconstruction in the limited sense that I had used its terms and aped its methods? Or was the lesson of the sign that our selves and our opposites are in some sense equivalent and interchangeable—and that therefore the deconstructive reversal of binary oppositions is always theoretically justified? The sign constituted a

*AWP Chronicle,* December 1992.

brilliant brief in favor of the intentional fallacy—the notion that the author's stated intentions may be disregarded by the reader—since "David Lehman, deconstructionist" would ambiguously mean or imply all these paradoxical things, whatever the intentions of the person who designed the sign, who might, after all, have been someone who was chiefly interested in graphic design and was not quite up to speed about who was doing what to whom in today's battles of the books.

In sum, we are at liberty to read the sign in various ways: as a mark of sarcasm, as evidence of casual ignorance, or as an object lesson in mediation and distortion, an example of what happens when reality is reduced to slogans and sound bites. The paradox of the sign may remind you of Freud's essay "The Antithetical Sense of Primal Words," in which Freud explores the notion that a single word originally stood for a thing and its opposite—that one word meant both *light* and *dark*. The incident reminded me of the joke about the Communist rally in front of the New York Public Library in the thirties. Demonstrators were clashing with counterdemonstrators when the police arrived and started busting heads indiscriminately. "But I'm an anti-Communist," said one man. "I don't care what kind of Communist you are," the cop replied, swinging his stick.

*Signs of the Times: Deconstruction and the Fall of Paul de Man* has occasioned a considerable amount of response, some of it passionate and provocative, much of it unusual. While nothing else has been quite as tersely ironic as that sign on the wall of Christ Church College in Oxford, a number of correspondents have found inventive ways to express their appreciation of the topsy-turvy logic of deconstruction. I particularly enjoyed the missive from the British professor with an Australian address who thought I had done a "nice demolition job" and added that it "couldn't happen to a nicer bunch of guys." The professor's lack of fondness for deconstruction did not, however, prevent him from catching the spirit of the enterprise for his own parodic purposes. He was mindful of the importance of erasure as a deconstructionist maneuver, the habit of printing a word or phrase in canceled form to produce an effect of skepticism even more pronounced than that caused by the liberal use of quotation marks. The procedure is known as putting something *sous rature*, or "under erasure." My correspondent printed the words "under erasure" in block capitals with a horizontal line running through them, indicating that the time was right to put *sous rature sous rature*. Then he advanced the theory that deconstruction had caught on in America but not in England because American pencils have erasers on them and British pencils do not. "It's all a matter of the material base," he winked, using, in that last phrase, the lit-crit code word for the flesh-and-blood reality that tends, in an age of theory, to get reduced to the marks on a chalkboard awaiting the eraser monitor's fresh wet sponge.

At the other extreme from the professor with the pencil-eraser theory was the angry fellow who charged that I hadn't read anything before writing *Signs of the Times*. I had considered using the occasion of this speech to refute the charge by proving that I had in fact read something. But then on second thought I decided to let it rest, for it seems a supreme compliment to me to suppose that I could write my book—replete with quotations from numerous sources—out of whole cloth, without recourse to other books and without the benefit of an assistant. To think I could do all that on the strength of my imagination alone! It's a positively Borgesian notion. Really, my critic does me too much honor. I may be clever, but I'm not *that* clever. A poet who *is* that clever, on the other hand, is John Ashbery, who—when asked at a cocktail party about Michel Foucault and poststructuralism—replied that he hadn't read Foucault and knew nothing about poststructuralism. Later that evening, when the conversation returned to the subject of Foucault, Ashbery made some incisive observations, and his interlocutor said, I thought you didn't know anything about Foucault, and Ashbery replied, "Well, I don't, but I *have* gone to cocktail parties."

As the fortunes of deconstruction as an academic phalanx have declined, and most observers will grant that they have, the chief sign of deconstruction—the word "deconstruction" itself—continues to proliferate in American culture at large. Just as existentialism in America seems to have more to do with attitude than with philosophy—suggesting the state of mind of someone who wears sunglasses in the subway and digs Miles Davis—so deconstruction seems to suggest, in popular parlance, the sum of its verbal parts: the threat of destruction and the suspicion that virtually anything is a con game, a candidate for debunking, including the activity of debunking itself. It is a pleasure to watch the word enter the public lexicon, for it illustrates with a fine irony the deconstructive precept that words are signs that escape the design that authors would impose on them.

In 1991, the BBC produced a short documentary on the de Man affair that begins with a pseudopunk band on the soundtrack singing "I want to destroy you," while "Waldheimer's Disease" made the list of new words and phrases tracked by the *Atlantic Monthly*. *Chicago* magazine devoted a cover story to "deconstructing twelve great evenings on the town." *New York* deconstructed David Duke. Deconstruction Records, a European dance music label, joined with RCA in releasing the twelve-song dance compilation *Decoded and Danced Up—Rhythms of Deconstruction* ("with tracks from hit artists like Black Box, N-Joi, and Guru Josh"). "Essays on deconstruction theory are written by people with pins in their necks," observed the poet Robert Bly, author of the best-selling book *Iron John* and leading guru of the burgeoning men's movement. Bly recalled a Russian fairy tale about a boy whose wicked stepmother—in cahoots with the boy's tutor—puts him to sleep by inserting a magic pin in his neck. When the boy wakes up he may find himself "isolated in a high mental tower." For Bly the tutor represents the educational system "right up through graduate school, [which] is in collusion with the dark side of the Great Mother." The pin stands for a "false phallus." Bly's message is clear: real men don't write essays on deconstruction theory.

There has been more of the same in 1992. Philip Johnson's architectural firm declared bankruptcy, and *Newsweek* headlined the story "Deconstruction."[1] The word turned up in Woody Allen's movie *Husbands and Wives:* Gabriel Roth, the Barnard professor of English played by Allen, remarks that a student of his has written a paper on "Oral Sex in the Age of Deconstruction." The word also appeared in several delightful cartoons by the *New Yorker*'s Stephanie Skalisky. In one of them, three persons are playing "Deconstructionist Scrabble." " 'Dog' spelled backward is 'god,' yet I still get the same number of points," muses one of the players. Another looks at the configuration of letters on the board and asks, "Is it only a word?" The third player wonders what the blank tile "really" represents.

Jacques Derrida was much in the news this year. Outraged dons at Cambridge University protested the awarding of an honorary doctorate to Derrida.[2] At Cornell University, by contrast, Derrida could count on a cordial reception for his two-part lecture "Is My Death Possible?" This witty title made me think of the philosophical cab driver in *The Maltese Falcon* who tells Sam Spade that he may not live forever, but "just the same, it'll always be a surprise to me if I don't."

On the intertextual front, a couple of Yale-trained critical theorists urged me to consider the parallels between de Man and Arthur Dimmesdale, the adulterous minister in *The Scarlet Letter*. I took the bait and can report that it is indeed a rare pleasure to read Hawthorne's great narrative with the case of Paul de Man fresh in one's mind. The chapter entitled "The Interior of a Heart" is particularly to the point. Dimmesdale is described there as a "subtle, but remorseful hypocrite," whose moral failings can by de Manian analysis be ascribed to his linguistic predicament. Dimmesdale longs to make a public confession. He tries to utter "the black secret of his soul." Yet even when he calls himself "the worst of sinners, an abomination, a thing of unimaginable iniquity," his statement—lacking any and all particulars of his adulterous affair with Hester Prynne—reinforces the general belief in his saintliness and humility. In short, the more Dimmesdale confesses, the less he is believed, and thus he aptly illustrates de Man's theory of confession, which may be thought a bankrupt rhetorical form to the extent that it rewards eloquence rather than sincerity.

Discussing Rousseau's *Confessions*, de Man analyzes the incident in which Rousseau relates having stolen a ribbon and blamed the theft on an innocent serving girl. De Man's point is that Rousseau's belated confession, whether heartfelt or not, wins him absolution and sympathy. The very rhetoric of confession guarantees the results. And as there is no way to tell a con artist from a repentant sinner, *confession* as a mode—like *sincerity* as a value—has been deconstructed. When confronted with the posthumous shock of de Man's youthful anti-Semitism on the one hand, and the fact that he never publicly confronted his collaborationist past on the other, de Man's followers sought not only to minimize the former but to excuse the latter, and they did so by maintaining that the master had been too fastidious to confess. In this way de Man's followers resembled Dimmesdale's in *The Scarlet Letter*. They had "heard it all, and did but reverence him the more"—either because zealots prefer to remain deluded about their charismatic paragons of virtue or because, in de Man's words, guilt "can always be dismissed as the gratuitous product of a textual grammar or a radical fiction." Well, it *is* tempting to regard Paul de Man as a version of the hypocritical clergyman who wants to appease his guilty conscience, lacks the courage to do so, and so (as Hawthorne writes) gains only "one other sin, and a self-acknowledged shame, without the momentary relief of being self-deceived." Still, other "intertextual" possibilities should be kept in mind as well. One of de Man's former students told me that she had always associated de Man with the Vichy police inspector, all cynicism and charm, played by Claude Rains in *Casablanca*. "Shocked! I'm shocked to find that there is gambling going on here," he says, pocketing his winnings, in Rick's Café Américain.

### The Politics of Deconstruction

In an early chapter of *Signs of the Times*, I explain the three most popular theories that people trot out to account for deconstruction's meteoric rise in America. Two of the theories—what I call "the Zeitgeist theory" and "the professionalism theory"—need not detain us here. But the third—let us call it "the sixties theory" or, perhaps, "the revenge-of-the-sixties theory"—is what I want to take a few minutes to consider, for it raises the whole issue of the politics of deconstruction. The theory has it that there is a more or less direct relation between the rebellious spirit of the sixties and deconstruction today. A lot of people seem to credit this notion—it is a commonly held, if unexamined, assumption. We are expected to nod our heads in casual assent without looking too closely at how it is supposed to have happened that radical campus politics at places like Berkeley and Columbia in the sixties was alchemically transmuted into the esoteric practice of deconstruction that the disciples of Paul de Man learned at Yale in the seventies.

The broad analogy makes a loose and easy kind of sense: deconstruction is to traditional literary criticism as an SDS takeover of buildings is to the normal functioning of a university—that is, both are revolutionary, at least in aspiration. Both are certainly disruptive. That statement, however, merely explains why the one phenomenon could serve as a ready metaphor or simile for the other, and it is possible that the linkage between deconstruction and the campus uprisings of the 1960s is primarily or even purely a function of rhetoric. If you took the trope literally, it might be a little more difficult to assent to the proposition that the unshaven seekers of utopia—the experimentalists in marijuana and free love, the celebrators of instinct and the body, the champions of vegetarianism and nude swimming, not to mention the metropolitan ironists and the cool practitioners of pop art—went back to campus at some point between George McGovern's crushing defeat and the kidnapping of Patty Hearst and, having failed to alter the social world, decided to take over the English department by espousing supercerebral French ideas that would "subvert the dominant paradigm," reduce the floating castle of metaphysics to the molecular particles of the air, and shake the institutions of literary criticism to their roots.

There were always too many missing links in this causal chain, always something glib about the theory that had the antiwar protesters of the Vietnam-era "sublimating" their political impulses and their rage into the fearsome technical apparatus of textual apparatchiks committed to the dismantling of canons of knowledge, taste, and judgment. The political suasion of deconstruction is far more ambiguous, far more questionable, than this scenario allows. The apocalyptic nihilism that is consistent with deconstruction, to the extent that it can be regarded as a distinctive aspect of the sixties, is not one that should be idealized. On the contrary, it seems to me more and more that deconstruction was not and is not an extension of the sixties but a betrayal of the best energies of that much misunderstood decade. The propensity of deconstructors to use their method to invert common hierarchies—such as truth and falsehood, or the literal and the figurative, or sanity and madness—has, in the end, more in common with the imperatives of a different decade and a different year—with George Orwell's *1984* rather than with the Kennedy years and the years of protest and upheaval. Though the deconstructionists claim that their method is a weapon to be directed against totalitarianism, it is indeed possible that the political system most consonant with deconstructive principles is authoritarian, whether of the Left or of the Right.

Anyone who doubted that deconstruction could serve the dictates of doublethink need only consider the defenses of Paul de Man that his disciples disseminated after the news of his wartime collaborationism broke. Suddenly, writers who ordinarily insist on the deep covert political agenda of a cultural event found themselves arguing that de Man's blatantly anti-Semitic line was really almost benevolent when you took a deconstructive whack at it. Geoffrey Hartman soft-pedaled the wrong de Man had done by "contextualizing" it. He insisted on "distinctions": de Man may have been a fascist, and he may have written an anti-Semitic article or two, and he may have given aid and comfort to the Nazi occupants of Belgium, but what he wrote was less hateful than what others had written, and besides, Hartman questioned "the link between fascism and the Holocaust," and then he lectured the reporters on the case for not reading enough books about fascist ideology.

In the pages of *Salmagundi*, meanwhile, John Sturrock reduced the whole of de Man's offense to one anti-Semitic article—conveniently overlooking the many others in which he had called for collaborationism as an immediate necessity and praised the German "revolution." Sturrock maintained that "anti-Semitism should not be criminalized," that expressions of anti-Semitism were not "physically injurious," and that de

Man's youthful anti-Semitism in particular "had nothing what-ever to do with the matter" of his "exemplary" criticism.

According to many deconstructionists, the popular con-demnation of de Man reflected just about everything except sincere moral outrage: resentment, *Schadenfreude,* and (in Hartman's words) "an opportunistic whittling down of decon-struction's reputation." But the deconstructors' response to their critics—whose motives they impugned and whose intel-lects they belittled—was paranoid enough to get them all the enemies they ever wanted.

Derrida introduced the argument that de Man's piece was covertly a critique of the more extreme articles in the same newspaper on that March day in 1941. Other de Man loyalists retreated to the "separation of realms" argument—that what de Man did then and what he taught later fell into two abso-lutely separate categories. If there is one position that the de Man affair absolutely debunks, it is this one, for the very issues that obsessed de Man in his theoretical work are raised by the biographical disclosures, and to say that there is no connection between them is unworthy of a serious student of human affairs.[3]

De Man published "The Jews in Contemporary Literature" in *Le Soir,* the daily newspaper with the widest circulation in Belgium, at the height of the Nazis' anti-Semitic propaganda campaign in March 1941—just a month before the Belgian equivalent of Kristallnacht took place. In this piece de Man argued that European culture was essentially healthy—the Jews hadn't "polluted" it. Yes, de Man wrote, the Jews *had* "played an important role in the phony and discorded exis-tence of Europe since 1920." But Jewish writers were unremit-tingly second-rate, and thus (he concluded) "a solution to the Jewish problem that would lead to the creation of a Jewish colony isolated from Europe would not have, for the literary life of the West, regrettable consequences. It would lose, in all, some personalities of mediocre worth."

I do not want to exaggerate the significance of what de Man did in articles like this one. He was certainly not in the position to do the harm done by his uncle, Hendrik (or Henri) de Man, close adviser to the king of Belgium and head of the Belgian Workers party, who urged his countrymen to collaborate with the Nazi invaders and to imitate them. No, Paul de Man was not quite the quisling that his uncle was. But in the face of repeated attempts to minimize the gravity of de Man's wartime writing, let this simply be said: had it not been for people who could speak calmly and reasonably about the possible consequences—which "need not be regrettable"—of mass deportations of Jews, the trains to Auschwitz would not have run with the damnable efficiency of the Nazis' final solution.

Derrida, in his deconstruction of de Man's anti-Semitic essay, made a major blunder. It is one thing to apply your method to a recondite and difficult text by an eighteenth-century philosopher or a German romantic poet; few will find you out if you are reckless or extravagant in your application of the method. But "The Jews in Contemporary Literature" resembles an op-ed column in length and manner, and its plain sense is as easy for us to grasp as it was for the Belgian population reading it in 1941. Yet here was Derrida suggesting, then insinuating, then implying, then not denying, then all but saying—in that maddening roundabout way of his—that de Man's piece subverted its own intentions and led the reader to an aporia, or a terminal ambiguity, with the effect that "The Jews in Contemporary Literature," was, no matter what it seemed to say, really a critique of "vulgar anti-Semitism." In one breath Derrida pardoned de Man for his pro-Nazi writings, and in the next he accused the journalists writing about de Man of employing Nazi tactics. It was, by twisted logic, they who were guilty of "the exterminating gesture." The world of deconstruction was a topsy-turvy one, all right.

Richard Rand of the University of Alabama, one of Derrida's translators, went even further than Derrida. He argued that de Man was actually the Jew in the case and that deconstruction was the victim of anti-Semitism.

It sounds ludicrous, but this is in fact what Rand argued, making one of those binary reversals that come as second nature to initiates into the mysteries of deconstruction. I suppose in a way I should be grateful to Rand for inadvertently providing me with an instance of academic absurdity that no satirist could have invented. In a nutshell he has shown that deconstruction can produce effects disastrously similar to those of the big lie in propaganda.

Whenever somebody says that deconstruction is a benign political phenomenon, I recall the conclusion of an essay on "The Deconstruction of Politics" by a professor aptly named Bill Readings in a book entitled *Reading de Man Reading*—a collection of essays infused with the spirit of devotion to Paul de Man. "American pluralism is as totalitarian as Stalinism," Readings writes. That is a scary proposition. Nor am I comforted by J. Hillis Miller's jolly statement, in his book *The Ethics of Reading*, that "the millennium [of universal peace and justice] would come if all men and women became good readers in de Man's sense." This hyperbolic claim, put forth so unironically by such an aggressive salesman for an idea, now sounds merely fatuous. But I can imagine circumstances in which it would have an ominous ring.

After the de Man affair, deconstruction will never again be a harmless thrilling thing—we have seen how it can be used to fudge facts, obfuscate truths, distort, and mislead. It cannot but be anathema for those of us who believe that there are true and false versions of a historical event, and that it is possible to distinguish between them. A few years ago, the "end of history" became a journalistic cliché overnight and was forgotten the next day, for history is what we continue to believe in, and by "we" I mean those of us who read and write for publication, who believe in accepting the moral responsibility for our words, and who have every reason to be profoundly suspicious of the deconstructionist party.

### In Theory

Is deconstruction finished? Funeral bells could be heard last summer at the School of Criticism and Theory at Dartmouth College, where Harvard deconstructionist Barbara Johnson gave a public lecture on "The Wake of Deconstruction." Other signs, too, suggest that the herd may stampede from the broken corral. An article by Jeffrey Nealon in the October 1992 issue of *PMLA* declares that deconstruction "is dead in literature departments today." My reaction to these pronouncements is skeptical. If deconstruction in the narrow sense is dead, its moment past, theory remains supreme in academe, and I maintain that the character of the Age of Theory was largely defined by deconstruction.

There is this to be said for theory: it can be extravagantly intoxicating in a way that is related to the raptures of poetic composition. And here I must acknowledge a certain ambivalence of my own. In both my poetry and my prose, I have demonstrated my affinity for the kind of wordplay and creative misreading that deconstructionists esteem. A mischievous maker of bilingual puns might even argue that the title *Signs of the Times* is a deliberate mistranslation of *Sein und Zeit*, the title of a major tome by Martin Heidegger; the English word "sign"—so crucial a term in literary theory—can be seen as a misprision of the German word for "being," *Sein*. As a poet, I know that I can count on language to generate its own meanings—that puns, unfairly derided as a low form of humor, can act as inspired figures of speech—and that typos and other seeming accidents can decisively alter the direction of a poem. One thing that attracts me to the sestina as a verse form is the opportunity it affords to collaborate with language. The poet is so busy working on the design of a sestina—getting the six end words to repeat themselves in the desired position and order—that he or she is unable to interfere with the signs and symbols flashing from the unconscious, which is but another (and perhaps needlessly clinical) name for the psyche, the memory, or the soul. I use words such as "self" and "soul" by design, to signal my stubborn attachment to concepts that have presumably received dishonorable discharges in the courts-martial of academic discourse. I like other unfashionable abstractions, too—freedom, art, genius, greatness. And so I have enlisted in the resistance to deconstruction—even as I concede that some of the tactics and procedures of deconstruction, if used judiciously, may lead to fruitful ends.

In *Signs of the Times* I make a limited case for what I call soft-core deconstruction, admittedly an elastic concept, and I am far from unaware of the creative pedagogical purposes to which it can be practically applied. In my own reading I keep encountering instances of deconstruction *avant la lettre*—as when Nietzsche, in *The Birth of Tragedy,* inverts the usual relation between walking and sleeping, consciousness and the unconscious. "Though it is certain that of the two halves of our existence, the waking and the dreaming states, the former appeals to us as infinitely preferable, more important, excellent, and worthy of being lived, indeed, as that which alone is lived—yet in relation to that mysterious ground of our being of which we are the phenomena, I should, paradoxical as it may seem, maintain the very opposite estimate of the value of dreams," wrote Nietzsche, anticipating what might be called Freud's deconstructions of the psyche.

Or consider the deconstruction of philanthropy begun by Charles Dickens and completed by George Bernard Shaw. In *The Mystery of Edwin Drood,* his unfinished last novel, Dickens skewers the character he calls Mr. Honeythunder, who occupies an office in London's "Haven of Philanthropy." The loathsome Mr. Honeythunder is not simply a hypocrite; he is, Dickens informs us, precisely the opposite of what he proclaims himself to be. He is, in Dickens's words, one of those who go "on errands of antagonistically snatching something from somebody, and never giving anything to anybody." The philanthropist turns out to be a misanthrope in disguise. Shaw in *Major Barbara* goes further, offering a kind of proleptic defense of the military-industrial complex and a kind of proleptic attack on the welfare state, when he endorses his heroine's switch of allegiance from the charitable offices of the Salvation Army to her father's munitions factory.

In English literature, Oscar Wilde is the greatest forerunner of deconstruction. Many of Wilde's merriest paradoxes are designed precisely to reverse some hierarchy or other. In particular he reverses the roles we usually assign to "truth" and "lie," "nature" and "art," "sincerity" and "style," "seriousness" and "triviality." In all these pairs, the first term is customarily valued to the disparagement of the second. Yet here is Wilde making a plausible defense of falsehood, in *The Decay of Lying,* in which he associates lying with poetry and art.

Wilde memorably deconstructs mimesis in the same work. He shows that the mirror held up to nature is two-sided. "Life imitates Art far more than Art imitates Life," he writes, and the statement may seem simple common sense to us today, aware as we are of copycat criminals, assassins inspired by the movies, elected officials who rely on memorized movie dialogue, and so forth. "In matters of grave importance, style, not sincerity, is the vital thing," says Gwendolen in *The Importance of Being Earnest,* offering the perfect one-sentence exposition of a whole aesthetic movement. *The Importance of Being Earnest* did have a "philosophy," Wilde declared—namely, "that we should treat all the trivial things of life seriously, and all the serious things of life with sincere and studied triviality." This "philosophy" seems to govern deconstruction as well. All you need to do is to translate "trivial" as "marginal," and "serious" as "central," and you will see the extent to which Wilde, tossing off his witticisms, accurately prefigured the perverse paradoxes and reflexive reversals of deconstruction.

Oliver Stone's *JFK,* unquestionably last year's most controversial movie, is both a murder mystery and an inspired instance of soft-core deconstruction: an exercise in speculation, a pure product of the age of theory. The movie is charged with a deep and affecting nostalgia for the early sixties. It is informed by a vision of America's recent political history so chillingly paranoid yet so plausible that it leaves one's mind in a state of high commotion. The cinematic techniques on display—the splicing together of actual black-and-white footage and ersatz newsreel, for example—succeed in blurring boundaries in the prescribed deconstructive fashion, and the movie certainly qualifies as a deconstruction of history. Ronald Steel in the *New Republic* called the picture "a deconstructionist's heaven," on the grounds that Stone shuttles back and forth from documentary history to pure speculation without warning the viewer which is which. As a result, Steel writes, "Every event becomes pseudo-event, fictions become fact, imagination becomes reality, and the whole tangible world disappears."

*JFK* would debunk the official version of President Kennedy's assassination in favor of a grandiose conspiracy theory at the highest levels of the military-industrial complex. Stone wants us to consider Kennedy's death as a repetition of the plot to kill Julius Caesar in Shakespeare's play—only here the culprits are not Brutus and Cassius but a wide range of spooks and cutthroats, anti-Castro Cubans, beefy military men, and (as an accessory after the fact) Lyndon Johnson. Their motives are said to include the Vietnam War. On the basis of little evidence, Stone plays his hunch—for which he has been roundly rebuked—that Kennedy was planning to withdraw American troops from Southeast Asia and that his political enemies could not tolerate such a reversal of policy.

Vietnam as a primary motive for Kennedy's assassination seems farfetched, and Stone is on safer ground—and his movie more profoundly disturbing—when he suggests that Kennedy committed the unforgivable sin by refusing to wage war on Cuba either during the aborted Bay of Pigs invasion in 1961 or during the weeks and months culminating in the Cuban Missile Crisis in October 1962. Historians regard the Cuban Missile Crisis as an unequivocal American triumph. President Kennedy made Premier Khrushchev blink in their eyeball-to-eyeball confrontation: the United States imposed a "quarantine" around Cuba, and as a result the Soviets removed their missiles and ended the immediate threat to our shores. Thus defined, the encounter was an undoubted triumph of American nuclear brinkmanship. But say—as Oliver Stone's movie does—that America's foreign policy objectives were defined differently; say that the nation's *real* foreign policy, the one to which American power was committed as opposed to the one offered for window dressing, was to overthrow Castro and liberate Cuba from Communism. Then the whole sequence of events admits of a diametrically opposite interpretation. One could contend, simply by flip-flopping the causal link between events, that the Soviets didn't back down at all—that they removed their missiles from Cuba after exacting from the Kennedy administration the agreement to abandon the foreign policy initiatives to which powerful American institutions and individuals, in the government and outside it, were dedicated to the point of hysteria.[4]

It seems to me that paranoid speculations based on a great

"what-if" may make for exhilarating novels and movies—
though they might well be out of place, and have a pernicious
effect, in works that advertise themselves as nonfiction, criti-
cism, history. If the power of *JFK* survives even the knowledge
that the filmmaker has stretched a point here and ignored
evidence there, it can be only because the movie exists for us
in the region of art, that privileged space where with perfect
liberty unthinkable thoughts may be rehearsed. Again, then,
my position is suitably paradoxical: I am upholding a tradi-
tional hierarchy—the one that distinguishes between art and
actuality, or between fiction and nonfiction—in the teeth of a
deconstructive assault on these distinctions, and yet at the
same time I can announce my provisional approval of the
deconstructive tactics that the filmmaker has appropriated for
his ends.

My last example of soft-core deconstruction is taken from
a headline last spring in the *Weekly World News,* a scandal-
sheet tabloid on sale near the supermarket cash register. The
headline:

Hitler Dead of Heart Attack

And just below that, in slightly smaller type:

Nazi Madman Buried in Buenos Aires

If headlines are the haiku of journalism, this is a brilliant
example. "Hitler Dead of Heart Attack" is obviously superior
to "Hitler Lives," since the former implies the latter—implies
that the postcentenarian Hitler was, contrary to received opin-
ion, alive until quite recently. But also, and more important,
"Hitler Dead of Heart Attack" deconstructs journalism itself
simply by being timeless—it could have run on any day since
April 30, 1945, the day that Hitler is thought to have commit-
ted suicide. The headline thus takes one of journalism's cardi-
nal maxims, that today's news is not yesterday's or tomor-
row's, and explodes it. And by being in itself worthy of critical
treatment, the headline makes the further point that a periph-
eral cultural artifact, like a supermarket tabloid, may allow us

to get at something more vital and central—in this case, the idea that Hitler is our anti-Christ, who must be ritually revived and killed again and again—as if history, our history, began with his death in 1945. Stephen Brockmann makes this argument in his essay "The Cultural Meaning of the Gulf War," in the spring 1992 issue of *Michigan Quarterly Review:* "Time, since 1945, is the constant refighting of the war which came to an end *in* 1945; and the constant attempt to definitively kill the false Messiah who killed himself in that year, thus transferring upon the whole world his sins and making any kind of a trial impossible." Brockmann tracks down ritual invocations of Hitler, such as President Bush's comparison of Saddam Hussein to Hitler, and explains their logic. "Hitler is alive, my enemy is alive, ergo my enemy is Hitler," Brockmann writes. "Since all these sentences are equations. . . , they can be reversed at will: Hitler is my enemy, my enemy is alive, ergo Hitler is alive. The system is closed and self-sufficient. Everything in it refers to everything else, and all statements say exactly the same thing."

If theory in the sense of speculation can trigger off a pleasurable mental commotion, I am far less sanguine about moves that would elevate theory at the expense of such of its antonyms as "conviction" or "seriousness" or "practice." In the writings of Stanley Fish, criticism turns into credentialism, and literature is reduced to something that pyramid-climbing professionals use to mount the staircase of institutional success. Fish argues with an arresting candor that the proper purpose of literary criticism is to advance the critic's professional career rather than to illuminate or evaluate literature as a good in itself or as a source of moral values. He would raise opportunism to an ideological position, and he would deconstruct criticism into a game with elaborate rules and annoying jargon. Is Fish a skeptic, a realist, or a cynic—or all three—when he maintains that one makes a name for oneself in academe by displays of calculated outrageousness?

Fish's debunking of the critic's trade makes him sound like Harold Bloom in a minor key and an antiheroic mode. In Fish's view, critics enjoy "the reverse of the anxiety of influence," because all they have to do is to invert the accepted view—no need to have the fearful struggle or *agon* that Bloom discerns in the growth of a great poet's mind. In *Is There a Text in This Class?* Fish provides the example of Jane Austen's *Pride and Prejudice*. The "Austen industry," in his phrase, runs on the assumption that her novels are ironic. Therefore, the smart move would be to argue that they aren't—to show, for example, that Mr. Collins is the secret hero of *Pride and Prejudice*. Fish is certainly a learned and clever critic, whose own professional career has prospered to the point that the *New York Times Magazine* has recently favored us with a profile of "Duke University's 'politically correct' showman." But his chief operating principle—that the critic may and even should say things simply for effect and not because they're true—seems to me a simple abdication of responsibility.[5]

The marked absence of moral seriousness in a profession that cries out for it is dismaying—as is the literature professor's perverse indifference to actual works of art and literature. An unhealthy competition between poets and critics seems an inevitable by-product of the hegemony of theory. There is, of course, a structural enmity at work here: in the best of times, the poet is supposed to regard the critic as "the assassin of my orchards," in Frank O'Hara's phrase. In the past, however, it was clear that the duty of criticism was to engage with poetry, whereas today the idea of an autotelic criticism has taken hold. Anyone who has read Geoffrey Hartman's verse or Harold Bloom's attempt at a novel will understand why these gentlemen want us to elevate the status of criticism, for they are not going to reach the literary hall of fame on the basis of their own creative writing. I have no trouble accepting the notion that a work of criticism might become a primary text of literature, but hadn't critics better start by improving the quality of their own prose? Meanwhile, the terminology of critical theory has had a sometimes devastating effect on the several poets it has decisively influenced, and I myself am determined not to read poems that have the word *gnostic* in them.

Criticism in recent years has been greatly preoccupied with the problems of representation, of mimesis. Theorists have worried the question of whether anything can be known or communicated. The association of representation with distortion led long ago to an epistemological blind alley, for we daily do the things that it is theoretically impossible for us to do, and the use of criticism to prove that every utterance contradicts itself is a little like getting hung up on Zeno's paradox. Why bother? The arrow isn't supposed to arrive, but we'd be wise not to step between the archer and his target.

In my view, the task for critics at the present time is to rediscover the poetry and the prose fiction that they have been neglecting, while the task for theorists is to return to one of the initiating moments in the history of literary criticism— the expulsion of the poets from Plato's *Republic*. It will be remembered that in this dialogue Socrates, after making the case against poetry and poets, proclaims himself to be open-minded and invites others to dissuade him if they can. The invitation to debate Socrates and refute Plato on the value or harm of poetry has been taken up by critics ever since, from Aristotle to Sidney, from Shelly to Matthew Arnold, from Tolstoy to Lionel Trilling. Given the social and political realities of our moment—when literature, art, and belles lettres are under pressure in the marketplace and under intense scrutiny in governmental offices—it is the right time, I think, for critics and theorists to address themselves to the defense of literature and to define the function of literary criticism in relation to this pressing and abiding concern.

## NOTES

1. Zeman and Howard, "Deconstruction," p. 14. Using similar logic, a linguist at the University of New Hampshire named Rochelle Lieber decided that the literal meaning of the verb "to deconstruct" is "taking something to pieces." In the preface of her book *Deconstructing Morphology: Word Formation in Syntactic Theory*, Lieber advises her readers that she does not intend "any similarity here to the use of the term 'deconstruction' by contemporary literary critics such as Derrida."

2. It was the first time in twenty-nine years that a candidate for an honorary degree had met with such a response at the venerable institution. In the end, the anti-Derrida insurrectionists failed by a vote of 336–204, but the episode spurred the *Wall Street Journal* to declare,

"Cambridge Deconstructs Derrida." Michael Miller, "A Mazy Grace: Cambridge Deconstructs Derrida," *Wall Street Journal*, June 11, 1992.

3. Consider Jean François Revel's comments on the case of Martin Heidegger: "There are only two alternatives. Either Heidegger's political commitment is derived from his philosophy, and if so, that challenges the meaning of this philosophy; or it is not derived from it, and if a philosopher can make such a grave choice without any relation to his thinking, this can only prove the futility of philosophy itself" (Revel, *The Flight from Truth*, trans. Curtis Cate [New York: Random House, 1991], p. 371).

4. A new book, *The Missiles of October: The Declassified Story of John F. Kennedy and the Cuban Missile Crisis* by Robert Smith Thompson (New York: Simon and Schuster, 1992), makes this argument: "Secretary of State Dean Rusk claimed that we and the Soviets had stood eyeball to eyeball, and that they had blinked first; yet, as now declassified documents show, President Kennedy offered the Soviets a pledge not only to refrain from an invasion of Cuba but also to remove from Turkey American missiles that Moscow said it found frightening" (15).

5. When I made this argument at the School of Criticism and Theory at Dartmouth in the summer of 1993, Barbara Johnson asked how I could know whether Fish made his remarks on *Pride and Prejudice* "for effect" or whether he meant them. Thus for the deconstructionist the discussion terminates in an undecidable *aporia,* an elegant dead end. For the rest of us, the epistemological quandary is far less compelling than the moral issue at hand.

# Derridadaism[1]

"Philosophy?
*Cela suffit!*"[2]
Said the man
Named de Man.[3]
J. Hillis Miller:
J. Phyllis Diller.[4]

---

1. Geoffrey Hartman's term in *Saving the Text.* An alternative spelling, *Derrida(da)ism,* subversively reveals the Russian *yes* within the demotic term for father.

2. The Saussurean *différence* between *Kant* and *cant* is blurred, deferred, and reinscribed in a Derridean display of *différance.*

3. A neglected trope, the paradigmatic palindrome deconstructs itself into a reversed binary opposition that terminates in an undecidable *aporia,* as when a pedestrian gets stuck in a revolving door (de Man's image).

4. One of several female pseudonyms employed by the late Benjamin Krull (1920–1986), university wit and author of some fifteen books including *The Deconstructive Prose Machine* (1985). Krull, who admitted to an "unreasonable admiration" for television comedienne Phyllis Diller, defined *phallogocentrism* as "what happens when you eliminate the space between the second and third words of the sentence *the pen is mightier than the sword.*"

*Times Literary Supplement* (London), May 18–24, 1990.

# From Disclosure to Closure

At Cambridge University in 1972, to write (as I did, to fulfill one of my tripos requirements) a long essay on the detective novels of Dashiell Hammett and Raymond Chandler and their relation to "serious" literature was considered an unusual thing to do. At the time, dons still put on pseudonyms when fashioning homicidal riddles in country houses. The genre remained vaguely disreputable, and that, I think, helped explain its "subversive" ability, which present-day professors of popular culture value so highly. Today, of course, an academic study of crime fiction in the context of serious literature can scarcely be thought novel, daring, or "subversive." The benefits of this situation are obvious, since "high" and "low" art can be shown to elucidate one another admirably. The mysteries of the mystery form deserve a critical treatment as ingenious and entertaining as our favorite stories.

In becoming academically respectable, however, the study of detective novels has acquired all the recurrent tics of contemporary scholarship: the slavish fidelity to fashionable French models, the theoretical bias, the jargon. In *Detective Fiction and Literature* Martin Priestman illustrates the pluses and minuses of the academic approach. He is sophisticated, has done his reading conscientiously, and is able to give a good running paraphrase of a complicated plot. He efficiently imparts received wisdom: the detective is the criminal's *doppelgänger; The Moonstone* should be viewed through a Freudian lens; Agatha

Review of *Detective Fiction and Literature: The Figure on the Carpet,* by Martin Priestman, published in the *Times Literary Supplement* (London), December 21–27, 1990.

Christie offers a version of pastoral, and so forth. Priestman has an excellent chapter on *The Valley of Fear,* the last of the Sherlock Holmes novels, and he has some suggestive things to say about the postmodernist infatuation with crime fiction. A naive affirmation of order, such as we get in thrillers of the Golden Age, "gives the relentlessly ironic postmodernist masters a classic model to be ironic about."

Priestman is capable of wit, as when he describes John Dickson Carr as a "pre-postmodernist" delighting quite candidly in his powers of artifice. But his prose is full of push-button formulations that do to language what inflation does to currency. When he says of Wilkie Collins's *The Moonstone* that it manages a "decentering of the controlling consciousness," what he means is that the book has multiple narrators. Sometimes the chitchat is up to date: you can deconstruct one critic's reading of *The Moonstone* by showing that his "emphasis on 'process' has an overall tendency to marginalise the novel's content." At other times, Priestman's jargon is reassuringly old hat: "It is worth asking whether the detective story is *specially* specialised in any way, in terms of content as well as form."

Invoking Roman Jakobson's distinction between metaphor and metonymy, Priestman maintains that Poe's tales of ratiocination are metonymic in structure while his tales of gothic horror are organized by the logic of metaphor. This strikes me as facile. Detective stories are invariably metonymic in the limited sense that the sleuth is forever extrapolating an entire scenario from a fragment, an action from a clue. But Priestman's argument that "the dominance of metonymy in detective fiction makes the genre fundamentally hostile to metaphor" is nonsense. What else is a locked room if not a metaphor? On some level Priestman realizes his error; he does, after all, refer to "The Murders in the Rue Morgue" as "a richly metaphorical psychodrama." In any event, the significant point about Poe's tales, whether they feature a detective or not, is how deeply metaphorical they are when compared with the efforts at naturalism that more properly illustrate the logic of metonymy.

"The Figure on the Carpet," Priestman's subtitle, is a nice touch, implying a comparison with Henry James's story. The

Jamesian protagonist, a literary critic, never discerns the secret message or buried treasure in the works of his favorite novelist. In contrast to the fictions of James or Conrad, the detective story proceeds from disclosure to closure. A valid point—though the allusion to James's title is a reminder that Priestman doesn't quite see the complex figure in the carpet when he looks at detective stories. What he sees as often as not is the back of another critic looking at the carpet hanging from the wall, whose clues are in full view of the public and are therefore perfectly hidden.

# The Heidegger Affair

Until a couple of years ago, Martin Heidegger's reputation as possibly the foremost philosopher of the twentieth century had suffered little damage on account of his membership in the Nazi party. People assumed that his Nazi fling was short-lived, half-hearted. Such rationalizations and evasions were no longer tenable after Victor Farias's book *Heidegger and Nazism* appeared in France in 1987 and in the United States two years later.

The evidence is overwhelming. Heidegger's philosophical investment in National Socialism lasted far longer than the year and a half he served as a rector of the University of Freiburg, enthusiastically enforcing Hitler's anti-Semitic decrees. He appears to have been a true believer, wild-eyed with ambition: he wanted to become the philosopher king of the Nazi state. As Jurgen Habermas, the German political philosopher, has written, Heidegger had "the nutty idea that he, as a spiritual leader, could set himself at the head of the whole movement. You have to be brought up in a German Gymnasium to have such notions."

The belated recognition that Heidegger's commitment to National Socialism was ideological and not merely opportunistic set off a furor in France, where the philosopher's ponderous texts have outlasted even Marxism as a galvanizing intellectual force. The controversy has also reverberated throughout Germany, where questions regarding collective memory and historical guilt are understandably an obsession, and in the United

Review of *The Heidegger Controversy*, ed. Richard Wolin, in *The Forward*, March 5, 1993.

States, where debates over the relationship between a thinker's biography and his thought have become particularly charged of late.

*The Heidegger Controversy,* an anthology of essays by and about Heidegger, documents the case against the philosopher and illustrates what the editor Richard Wolin describes as "the intellectual continuity between Heidegger's philosophical writings of the late 1920s and his pro-Nazi texts of the early 1930s." As rector of Freiburg, Heidegger toed the Nazi Party line, doctrinally and in administrative policy, and in the process betrayed old mentors and colleagues. He subscribed to the Nazis' cult of leadership, or *Fuhrerprinzip,* as well as to their racist blood-and-soil ideology. In his Rectoral Address in May 1933, he hailed "the glory and greatness" of Hitler's Germany. He concluded other speeches with "*Heil* Hitler!"

Heidegger claimed he became disillusioned with the Nazis on 30 June 1934, the infamous "Night of the Long Knives," when Hitler turned on his old pal, SA leader Ernst Roehm, and had him murdered. Victor Farias speculates that Heidegger was a "radical" Nazi in the manner of the brown-shirted Roehm, and it is possible that Heidegger came to rue Hitler primarily for giving National Socialism a bad name. In any case, the philosopher never did issue an unambiguous repudiation of the principles he adopted when he joined the Nazi party. He remained convinced of the "inner truth and greatness" of National Socialism, which he defined as a product of "the encounter between global technology and modern man."

Heidegger, who made few public statements that have any bearing on the Nazi period, in 1949 likened the manufacture of corpses in concentration camps to the mass production of agricultural goods. The analogy, in addition to being indecent, exposes a weakness not of character, or not *just* of character, but of moral philosophy. For the implication of the statement is that the blame for Nazi atrocities properly rests not with human beings but with the impersonal forces of technology, which Heidegger demonizes in his philosophy. It is not a way of thinking that allows for individual moral responsibility.

The MIT Press's paperback reprinting of Richard Wolin's anthology, which first saw the light of day as a Columbia University Press hardcover three years ago, is newsworthy for one twist of its publishing history. The original edition included an interview with Jacques Derrida, the grand wizard of deconstruction, that touched on the subject of Heidegger and the Nazis. The absence of the interview from the paperback—and, too, the change of publisher—are a direct result of M. Derrida's threat to bring legal action against the book. As chronicled by Thomas Sheehan in the *New York Review of Books*, this is a story rife with irony—an exhibit, in T. S. Eliot's phrase, of "human folly, and the laceration of laughter at what ceases to amuse."

The interview in question was conducted in French for *Le Nouvel Observateur* and was translated by Mr. Wolin for his anthology. Permission to reprint was granted by the periodical, as is customary. M. Derrida was not consulted, as he doubtlessly should have been (though the publication rights to an interview are usually thought to belong to the interviewer rather than to the person being interviewed). When he came upon Mr. Wolin's book in a shop, M. Derrida flew into a rage—and brought the pressure of his fierce rhetoric to bear on Columbia University Press and on Mr. Wolin, demanding that the interview be deleted from the paperback edition of the book, then in preparation. Mr. Wolin agreed but wanted to add a preface addressing the subject of his worsening relations with M. Derrida. Columbia balked; Mr. Wolin left, complaining about M. Derrida's "intimidation tactics," and MIT Press took over the project.

Why had M. Derrida gone to such lengths to suppress the publication of the interview—and of the book itself, if that turned out to be a consequence? The "interview was published without my authorization, in an execrable translation, and in a book that, as is my right, I judge to be weak, simplistic, and compulsively aggressive," he harumphed. But something else was bothering M. Derrida besides Mr. Wolin's deficiencies as a writer and translator: the editor had dismissed Derrida's complex but ultimately equivocal position on Heidegger, characterizing it as "far-fetched and illogical."

In academic debate M. Derrida is notorious for having a thin skin and a short fuse, yet each temper tantrum is always a little shocking in its violence, and the shrill contumely that he heaped upon Mr. Wolin's head (he accused him of "unbelievable, shocking and inadmissible behavior") was a bit much. The chief irony is that M. Derrida is supposed to have deconstructed authorial identity and intention, not to mention the bourgeois notion that the author is in some ways the owner of the text he produces. Yet he finds it easy enough to suspend his disbelief in these reviled notions when his own interests are at stake.

It is even possible that M. Derrida's ire is a smokescreen for what is, after all, an act of self-censorship. Trying to put a happy spin on things, Mr. Wolin suggests that M. Derrida is trying to distance himself from his "quasi-exoneration of Heidegger's philosophically overdetermined commitment to National Socialism"—a formulation that tells you all you need to know about Mr. Wolin's prose style.

To those who argue for a "separation of realms"—believing that a thinker's ideas and actions belong in irreconcilably separate categories—the Heidegger affair has dealt a tremendous blow. One can see why somebody would like to draw an artificial distinction between a life in history and the life of ideas—one can see the attraction of working in an abstract plane where no clerk ever committed treason. But the danger of this tendency is apparent. When they talk about the real world in faculty lounges these days, they call it "the quote-unquote real world." It's a place the professors of theory too seldom visit.

# Gettysburg, Deconstructed

What with the 1993 Pulitzer Prize going to Garry Wills's book about the Gettysburg Address, and now a four-hour cinematic epic depicting the battle that inspired Abraham Lincoln's greatest speech, you'd think that this, the noblest of American orations, is enjoying the high prestige it deserves—even in academe. Guess again.

A few weeks ago I lectured at Wittenberg University, a Lutheran campus in the heartland of Ohio. Copies of my book, *Signs of the Times: Deconstruction and the Fall of Paul de Man,* had been circulated ahead of my visit; I'd been asked to speak informally on the posthumous scandal surrounding the Yale guru of deconstruction, the academically trendy literary theory that sets out to prove that all texts are indeterminate, yield contradictory meanings, and can be construed to mean the opposite of what they say. De Man had, it turned out, written for pro-Nazi newspapers in his native Belgium during World War II.

Most of the questions raised in the q-and-a that followed my talk had little to do with my book, and much to do with "canon-expansion" and other politically correct shibboleths of the moment. One young woman, for example, spoke of the need to expand the literary canon by reducing the number of "dead white European males" on required reading lists in college courses. Then she said that "the founders of this country were white male racists." When I commented rather gently that this statement was as "absolute and totalizing" as anything that the jargon-spewing academics are supposed to deplore, a bearded

*Chicago Tribune,* February 11, 1994.

professor in a blue suit rose to her defense. To my surprise he cited approvingly the mock-deconstruction of the Gettysburg Address offered on pages 57 and 58 of *Signs of the Times* (he held up the book for emphasis).

"For the hard-line deconstructionist," I wrote, "any text, any system of signs, can be shown to compromise itself from within. Here, for example, is the opening of the Gettysburg Address: 'Fourscore and seven years ago our fathers brought forth on this continent a new nation, conceived in liberty, and dedicated to the proposition that all men are created equal.' Most of us will have no trouble construing this statement or its 'intertextual' relation to the Declaration of Independence, in which the phrase 'all men are created equal' also appears; Lincoln means to exalt equality as one of the nation's founding principles. A deconstructionist, however, might pause over 'our fathers brought forth' and 'conceived,' characterizing this trope as an attempt to appropriate for the patriarchal authorities the procreative power vested in the female body. 'All men are created equal,' but the deconstructionist might point out that 'men' excludes women and other 'marginalized' figures and that the document therefore promotes something other than full equality. 'Government of the people, by the people, for the people,' Lincoln urged, but the deconstructionist may argue—as H. L. Mencken once did—that it was actually the Confederate states that fought for self-determination. At work in such exercises is a kind of perverse imperative. The critic must expose the text as one would expose a scam or a sham, for all texts are presumed guilty, complicitous with a Western philosophical tradition that the procedures of deconstruction are designed to discredit."

It had not escaped Professor Davis, Bob Davis, the Berkeley-trained professor in the blue suit, that I had written these words in the effort to skewer and lampoon deconstruction, though he was probably unaware that the exercise had taken me all of twenty minutes, since I had just applied some basic deconstructive clichés to Lincoln's magnificent speech. But for Professor Davis (who, I found out later, runs Wittenberg's writing program) my mock-deconstruction was right on the mark. The Gettysburg Address *does* marginalize women and *does* appropriate for the patriarchal authorities the maternal power of the female body. What's more, said he, Abraham Lincoln was in fact a racist. We should, he added, interrogate our historical "texts." Why, he wanted to know, was it all right for me to deconstruct Paul de Man's pro-Nazi journalism—and why wasn't it all right for others to do the same to the Gettysburg Address?

In response I refrained from pointing out that what I had done to Paul de Man was a deconstruction only in a figurative sense. Instead I asked the professor whether he really saw no difference between Lincoln's great speech and de Man's crude journalism. I said the Gettysburg Address was not just a "great text." It is also an essential statement of this nation's principles: our dedication to liberty and equality not simply as privileges inherited but as "the great task remaining before us"; our resolve to conclude the Civil War with a "new birth of freedom." Was it pointless to mention that Lincoln had initially vaulted into national prominence because of his principled opposition to slavery? It was Lincoln who issued the Emancipation Proclamation freeing the slaves, Lincoln who campaigned for passage of the Thirteenth Amendment. Had Lincoln turned from the great emancipator into a racist by one of those deconstructive sleights-of-hand that make a thing merge with its own opposite?

The lesson is not that deconstruction, on the decline at places like Yale and Duke, is thriving at academic outposts like a lagging cultural indicator, working its mischief. We always knew that deconstruction is far from neutral or value-free; on the contrary, with its strategy of inverting oppositions and dismantling hierarchies, it fosters some of the worst excesses of political correctness. The real lesson is the sobering one about the atmosphere on campuses today, where a civil was is going on—bloodless, in fortunate contrast to the conflict that got fought out in places like Antietam and Shiloh and Gettysburg—but a peculiarly low and mean-spirited species of ideological warfare in which epithets like stinkbombs are hurled around wantonly and nobody does very much about the alarming, the truly terrifying ignorance that is rampant across our land. For the really sad thing is that the righteous students indoctrinated in deconstructive jive couldn't tell the Gettysburg Address from a Pennsylvania zip code.

Ignorance is general. It is disheartening to stare at blank faces when you stand in a classroom and mention Icarus, or Thucydides, or Job, or Dante, or Robespierre, or Schubert's Unfinished Symphony, or . . . the Gettysburg Address. We can either read the Gettysburg Address or we can deconstruct it—there isn't enough time to do both. We should beware of deconstructing the Gettysburg Address when the fact of the matter is that today we scarcely possess it.

If I were running the freshman writing program at Xanadu University I would require the students to memorize the Gettysburg Address. I would have them study it as oratory—to note how Lincoln uses the word *dedicate,* how he organizes his argument—but also as a statement of national purpose, a declaration of principles that we cannot simply take for granted but must reaffirm. I would dwell on the president's rhetorical mission, his effort to impose a meaning somehow commensurate with the carnage of the Civil War. And I would challenge the students to see what they could accomplish in 272 words—the length of the address Lincoln made to dedicate a cemetery on the site of a battlefield in a drizzling rainfall on November 19, 1863.

# Notes on Political Correctness

*Political correctness* has a history. Leninists used the phrase approvingly to indicate proper party-line behavior, though soon enough it was used against them to denote knee-jerk fidelity to the god that failed. The return of the phrase suggests that people active in the resistance to the new multicultural order discern in it yet one more variant on the old Marxist/Leninist model of radical social change.

Premise: political correctness is to the eighties and nineties what fellow traveling was to the thirties and forties. Is this rhetoric or is this truth? A bit of both. To the extent that it is an exaggeration, the analogy suggests the intensity of the anxiety provoked by multiculturalism. ("All of the passions lead to exaggeration," said Chamfort. "That is why they are passions.") But the analogy does have the virtue of logically conjoining two equally current academic phenomena: on the one hand, the battle over free speech on campus; on the other, the prevalence on campus of a nostalgically sentimental view of Marxism in general and "the New Left" in particular.

In retrospect it certainly seems that the seminal text for understanding the rise of political correctness is that New Left classic, Herbert Marcuse's *Critique of Pure Tolerance*. According to the revolutionary logic that countless campus cadres derived from Marcuse, tolerance was repressive. Deconstruct ethical values and norms of conduct such as tolerance, open-mindedness, civility, and courtesy, and these would be seen not as discourse-enabling virtues but as ruses that favor the perpetuation of the status quo. A policy of exclusionary

*Partisan Review,* Fall 1993.

intolerance was one way to trap the powers that be. The classic humanist would feel constrained to act in a manner accommodating to his adversaries; the insurgent, committed to an adversarial posture, would feel no such obligation. The former, by hiring the latter, would conspire in his own downfall.

What else is political correctness but a massive case of intolerance—the inability or unwillingness to tolerate a rival point of view? Since the whole tendenccy is in violation of the stated principles of free inquiry, the reign of intolerance is ever in need of theoretical justification. The latest attempt is by the attention-grabbing Stanley Fish in his book *There's No Such Thing as Free Speech, And It's a Good Thing, Too.* Upon such a rock is found the church of political correctness.

Political correctness stems from the drive to cast all matters of culture and intellect in political terms. Politics has triumphed in the academy to the degree that it is commonly accepted, without much dissent or debate, that everything from sexual behavior and the life of the nuclear family to the meaning of poems and paintings is political. Not only does everything have a political dimension; more emphatically, everything is primarily (and structurally) political before it is anything else. This includes the academic life. For Stanley Fish the field of literary studies is a place where professionals make career moves, jostling for power and glory, and it always was; all the big talk about morals and manners and how literature could change your life was always just talk, a sales pitch for suckers.

Defenders of the P.C. faith take it for granted that they have justice on their side. They tend to sound righteous, aggrieved. "I consider 'political correctness' to be a term created by the European American far right in order to maintain its position of power and privilege in this society, a position achieved by a long legacy of racial and sexual oppression," writes Velina Hasu Houston in her introduction to *The Politics of Life,* a collection of four plays by Asian-American women. Hers is the rhetoric of special pleading, the language of victimization, and it is routinely used in committee meetings when grants and fellowships in the arts are decided. It is used, for example, in arguments justifying quotas on the grounds that different (lower) standards apply to members of a disadvantaged group. Advocates of multiculturalism act as if a discussion of merit is beside the point in the case of a candidate with the right demographic credentials. Art for them is an instrument for progressive social change. They reject the idea that the value of art rests in its autonomy and independence, and set about proving that all art is "always already" political in some sense or other. Committee members critical of a work on the ground that it is meretricious or superficial or technically incompetent are themselves denounced on the ground that they are incapable of responding to the "non-linear" thinking or the "anti-Western metaphysics" in the work in dispute. This is smokescreen talk, owing something to warmed-over Derrida and other gurus of the moment. It is meant to disguise the fact that artistic works are being judged not by real critical criteria but by something else, something resembling touchy-feely boosterism.

It is assumed that the enlightened citizen of the intellectual world is highly political in nature, strongly leftist in orientation, and willing to purchase the whole package of contemporary academic opinion with its many deep prejudices and its deconstructive bent. The citizen is enlightened, in other words, to the exact extent that he or she holds the right opinions. If that is at the heart of political correctness, it is not exactly a novel phenomenon. Flaubert anticipated it (though not the specifically political form it has taken) in his *Dictionary of Received Ideas*.

The idea of systematically subjecting opinions, political and otherwise, to standards of correctness depends on a Manichaean conception of the social world: history consists of an unbroken series of incidents pitting victims and oppressors, us and them, the enlightened and the benighted. It is not terribly sophisticated; victims and villains are substituted for the heroes and bad guys in shoot-em-ups targeted for the preteen audience. This vision of a stark and simple dualism in the universe, this science of victimology, is one thing that Marxism has to offer. Taken together with other fashionable *isms* and *ologies* of our moment, it, the old reliable, can teach you how to line up unerringly on the right side of any given issue.

There is a plethora of Marxisms on college campuses, and they differ from one another in numerous particulars, but it seems as if each of them is conceived as a speculative model rather than as a series of wretched historical cases. Spreading from the English department to the social sciences and law faculties, the fetish of literary theory—the popularity of the idea that everything is finally textual—has helped foster an atmosphere in which the adept can avoid reckoning with the historical particulars that would wreck a utopian thesis. There is no truth; there is only discourse. Knowledge has little to do with fact, everything to do with theory. Thus the romance of the Left has continued unabated despite the fall of the Berlin Wall, the collapse of Communism in Eastern Europe, and the incontrovertible proof that Marxism in practice is ruinous economically and tyrannical politically, bringing nothing but misery to the peoples who have lived under its yoke.

The romance of the Left rests on that rusty old tenet of Romanticism, the identification of poverty with virtue. (Poverty had previously been associated with vice, as you can see if you check the etymology of words like "scamp" and "rascal.") Mary McCarthy, in *The Groves of Academe* (1952), describes a "true liberal" as one "who could not tolerate in her well-modulated heart that others should be wickeder than she, any more than she could bear that she should be richer, better born, better looking than some statistical median." There is something of this sentimentality in the behavior of the politically correct—as in, for example, their well-documented, much-lampooned deployment of euphemisms, which work by a process of linguistic wish-fulfillment, obfuscating inconvenient facts, so that "fat" becomes "circumferentially challenged" and "handicapped" turns into "handicapable."

Euphemisms are the placebos of language. The speed with which the politically correct bureaucrat will reach for one—or for the censor's scissors—implies a certain belief in the power of words, of rhetoric, to manage and to massage. Whoever controls the discourse, controls everything: the influence of Michel Foucault has been as considerable as that of Jacques Derrida.

A generous view: when idealism goes academic it turns into

ideology, and when ideology hardens into doctrine, political correctness results. The road to political correctness is paved with good intentions. A severe view: it is a symptom of bad faith and inauthenticity, and should be treated within the larger context of "the treason of the clerks." Ironist's view: the use of "diversity" to describe the politically charged atmosphere on college campuses proves the deconstructionist's point that a word can mean its own opposite. Educational reformer's view: political correctness is part and parcel of the entire syndrome of academic snobbism: the fear of being wrong, the terror of associating with one's intellectual inferiors. Academics decry hierarchies but have an acute awareness of them, which makes sense when you remember that their own institutional structures are among the most hierarchical in our society. The desire to please one's powerful elders comes as second nature to climbers of tenure ladders. If you really want to strike at the roots of political correctness, begin with a system that reduces assistant professors to sniveling grovelers—scrap tenure.

Premise: "correctness" has more to do with conformity than with a sense of rectitude. It is curious that the urge to conform should be so strong in the land of Emerson and Thoreau. It is doubly curious that professors who want to "teach students to think for themselves" should be so susceptible to an anxiety about being (or being thought to be) different. There is very little real deviation from accepted norms of thought in the academy. The self-styled radical is in actual behavior as much an organization man as the "other-directed" members of David Riesman's *Lonely Crowd*—a book written on the eve of the fifties. Yet valedictorians do laud the virtues of individualism and originality, and a great hue-and-cry will always be made over figures that seem to embody a "new" and putatively revolutionary spirit. The mimetic compulsion assures that any true or apparent maverick will instantly be copied; that the copies will circulate with terrific speed via the technological media; and that in time the ever-proliferating copies of copies will swamp the market denuded of whatever substance inhered in the original. It is all like a media junkie's version of the parable of Plato's cave. The process turns heroes into "role models" and, in the realm of ideas, reduces convictions into theoretical propositions to be entertained and abandoned. Intellectual discussion is definitely "academic" to the very extent that it is weightless, of no real consequence, running no risks.

When the long hair and beards of the sixties succeeded the crewcuts and flattops of the fifties, many thought that the change was a symbolic representation of a change in social values. When jocks of the seventies began to sport mustaches and filled the locker room with hair dryers, it was becoming clear that the hirsute revolution signaled a change in style only. The handlebar mustaches on the mug of an ace relief pitcher signified less than the mustache Marcel Duchamp contributed to the face of the Mona Lisa. But in time Duchamp's gesture was canceled out by its own ubiquitousness—it had been reduced to the status of a reproducible image, empty of meaning. The obsessive concern of American academic intellectuals with matters of style and fickle fashion seems irreversible. Back in 1972 Wendell Berry cited "an intellectual fashionableness" as an instance of the consumer mentality. "The uniformity of dress, hair style, mannerism, and speech is plain enough," he wrote. "But more serious, because less conscious and more pretentious, is an intellectual fashionableness pinned up on such shibboleths as 'the people' (the most procrustean of categories), 'relevance' (the most reactionary and totalitarian of educational doctrines), and 'life style.' "

The resort to political considerations in the context of the critical evaluation of works of art implicitly devalues art, though this is not usually acknowledged in the committee rooms of foundations and government agencies. Scholars, who can afford to be somewhat more candid, will grant that the emphasis on the political goes together with an antipathy to the moral and aesthetic dimensions of experience. In advanced circles, works of art are approached as cultural "products" deemed to be of interest because they reinforce certain political suasions and tendencies. Art requires demystification. It is a front, a camouflage, diverting the concerned citizenry from some sort of power play or ploy. It is as if works of art operated on principles akin to those of television commercials: paid for, they are charged with the task of propagandizing for a particular platform. And if art is no better than and no different from an editorial or an advertisement, how else to judge it except on the basis of the message it expresses or the political gesture it makes? The subordination of art to politics, almost always a sure-fire prescription for artistic disaster, is the risk run by high-minded philanthropic enterprises. When bureaucrats use art, culture, and higher education as the means to pursue agendas of social justice, the result may or may not be justice in the social sphere but it is almost inevitably mediocrity in the cultural sphere.

Political correctness is a socially acceptable form of old-fashioned prudery. The novelist Harry Mathews, discussing the politically incorrect attitudes of French male surrealists in the twenties and thirties, gives short shrift to readers who profess to be shocked by the sexism on display. "Its dreary humorlessness aside," Mathews writes, "the worst thing about political correctness is that it oppressively discourages telling the truth about one's ideas, sentiments and actions." And perhaps the next worst thing is that it condescends to people who had the misfortune of living in an era not nearly as enlightened as our own. It is bad faith to punish historical personages for breaking rules that had not yet been prescribed when they were alive. "What is persuasive in what the male surrealists have to say," writes Mathews, "is their unflagging commitment to veracity, no matter how embarrassing or shocking or self-demeaning its results may prove." This "commitment to veracity" is at the opposite extreme from the state of denial for which the politically correct euphemism is a screen.

The reign of intolerance and political correctness has had other consequences as well, many of them deleterious. Grade inflation by itself seems a minor enough thing to worry about until you remind yourself that it is a function of groupthink, closedmindedness, and a priori argumentation. "A lot of grade inflation in the humanities is due to the fact that many courses now have an ideological basis," observes Harvard professor William Cole. "Where once you had a course in, say, nineteenth-century French literature, now the course will be something like 'The Repression of Women by the Dominant Discourse of Nineteenth-Century French Literature.' Students who enroll will all agree with its premise, that literature acts in a certain way to marginalize women. It's curious that the same academics who most vociferously promote diversity wind up with the most monolithic classrooms. The teacher is surrounded not by students but by disciples. And hey—you give your disciples A's."

Overheard on a cactus university campus: "Historically," said the graduate student, "we've gotten to the point that irony is immoral." The attitude is unfortunate, but it is easy to understand. In dreary earnest, the politically correct tend to distrust the anarchic, uncontrollable impulses of mirth and humor. Irony and wit are casualties of this distrust. But irony is also the rhetorical trope for the attempt of the mind to accommodate conflicting points of view. The very phenomenon of political correctness militates against this trope, this habit of thought. The politically correct mind has had enough of complexity, nuance, contradiction, uncertainty, irony. The politically correct mind yearns to know where it stands and would seem to be willing to put up with tyrannical limitations on its own freedom—simply in order to enjoy the satisfaction of always being in the right.

# UNDER DISCUSSION
## Donald Hall, General Editor

Volumes in the Under Discussion series collect reviews and essays about individual poets. The series is concerned with contemporary American and English poets about whom the consensus has not yet been formed and the final vote has not been taken. Titles in the series include:

*Please write for further information on available editions and current prices.*

***Ann Arbor***          University of Michigan Press